PAINTING
THE LANDSCAPE OF
YOUR SOUL

A journey of self discovery

Damini Celebre

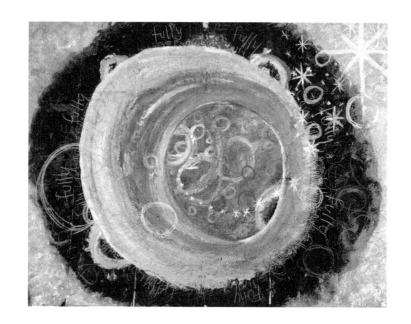

PAINTING
THE LANDSCAPE OF
YOUR SOUL

A journey of self discovery

Damini Celebre

Brushheart Press PENNSYLVANIA : NEW MEXICO

Invocation Prayer / Betsy Bergstrom

I give thanks to those that I am about to invite!

I ask that this room, this home or building and the grounds become a sacred space.

I invite the Divine to be present.

I invite Great Spirit, Mother Father God to be present.

I invite Great Mystery to be present.

I invite the Compassionate and loving Ancestors to be present and I give thanks to them, because without them we couldn't be here.

I invite the Great Teachers and Masters to be present, especially those that we have connections to and affiliations with.

I invite the Angels, the great beings of light, especially the Archangels, the guardian angels and the angels of healing.

I invite the Power Animals, the Totems, and I give thanks to them for loaning their power, their qualities and for relationship.

I invite the Healing Spirits of all the realms and give thanks for the healing that I know is going to happen.

I invite the Elements: Earth, Water, Fire, Air and Sacred Space...and I ask for a balancing of the Elements.

I invite the Compassionate Spirits and Devas.

I Invite the Earth, the Sun and the Moon.

I give thanks to the Stars and the Compassionate Star People.

I invite the Directions and the Guardians of the Directions

I invite the Four Great Winds.

I give thanks to the Great Spirits of the Land and I ask to be in harmony with you and to prosper here.

I give thanks to the Spirits of this place for allowing this work to happen here.

And as always, I give thanks in advance for the blessings that I know will happen here.

Thank you!

contents

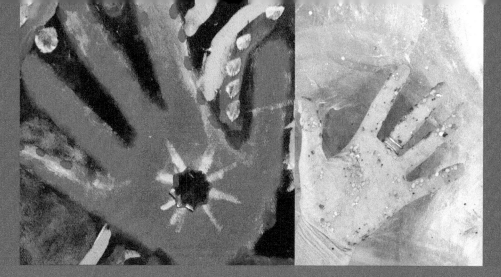

www.daminicelebre.com

Brushheart Press PENNSYLVANIA : NEW MEXICO

Foreword / Sandra Ingerman

It is our birthright to fully express our soul. We live in a time when many people feel a false safety in choosing to live in the status quo. Unfortunately, in childhood many of us were taught that there are only a few highly creative people and that you are not one of them. Most of us repress our creative fire. This repression has created an immense amount of physical, emotional, and mental illness. When we do not allow our creativity to flow we dishonor ourselves and life itself.

The "cure" is to allow the self-expression we yearn for to flow. In this book, you will start by becoming reacquainted with the language of color, shape, and form. Your creative voice will emerge as you learn to tap into the source of your creative self. We are all artists deep down inside. But we must change our definition of art. Art is expression that leads to action and change. We each have an artist inside of us waiting to be invited to create.

I love to paint. Painting has brought a lot of healing into my life, and it has been a fun experience for me to engage in. It is a way for me to play with color and express what is emerging from the depth of my soul.

Many years ago I was lucky to have a friend show me how painting is much more than creating a project that has an outcome. She taught me how I could allow free-form painting to be a time for healing and regeneration. I needed her encouragement. For in the past, I did not allow myself to do any artwork. I had high expectations and put pressure on myself, blocking the force of my creative spirit from shining through.

In *Painting the Landscape of Your Soul*, Damini Celebre will act as an encouraging guide for you. You need no prior creative experience to proceed with the material in this book. You just need a sense of curiosity, a desire to explore using painting as a way to reawaken your vital energy by tapping into the energy within you, as well as a desire to heal your past wounds. This book will open you to your creative life force with the goal of naturally allowing more of your vital energy to flow within and through you.

Damini leads you to explore your own creative nature, which will guide you to discover how you can interact in the world in new ways. She provides step-by-step instructions for using intuitive painting to express what is waiting in the depth of your soul. I love how Damini helps to create a safe place that holds and creates a container to witness, honor, and acknowledge your old wounds and allow your deepest desires to reveal themselves. This is done from a place of nonjudgment with the ultimate goal of feeling energetic and self-empowered. And the exercises she provides are fun to engage in.

Damini shared with me how her inspiration to write this book came to her during a meditation. In the past she had not entertained the possibility of writing a book. She did not see herself as a writer. But she felt strongly that she had much to share from her experience as an acupuncturist, shamanic practitioner, and artist. And as a true alchemist, she mixed the elements of her knowledge together to create a book that has many levels of teaching and wisdom woven into the exercises she shares. I am so delighted she followed her intuitive guidance to share with us this powerful book.

Painting the Landscape of your Soul is for those of you who are looking to discover and acknowledge the truth of who you are. It is for those of you who would like to commit to living a life filled with passion, meaning. The book is filled with guided exercises that lead you on a healing journey. These journeys will inspire you to express on paper any past experiences and information that need to be transformed and healed as you walk the path of living from your authentic self. Using the creative process as the foundation for self-discovery, you will learn to override limiting beliefs of your mind, connect to unlimited possibilities, establish a deep sense of trust with your intuition, and then learn to listen and follow your intuitive voice.

This book is a step-by-step journey of empowerment, reclaiming your inner self with paint on paper. Damini is a wonderful communicator. She has a great gift of being able to start at the beginning and clearly explain the deep underlying principles of energy medicine, shamanism, and expressive arts.

I have known Damini Celebre for over twenty years. She is a medicine woman who has a bright light shining through her eyes. I always appreciate her positive attitude and her enthusiasm. Damini is an adventurer and a free spirit. As I read the book I can perceive her free-spirited nature encourage and uplift readers to open up to the wonders of empowering yourself by opening up to your creative spirit.

Damini combined her two passions, creative arts and healing arts, to synthesize the unique approach to awakening your unique true self that *Painting the Landscape of Your Soul* presents. Damini brings her wealth of experience to the material. She began her career over thirty years ago, as a professional artist and educator. Twenty years ago, she began her practice as an acupuncturist and a shamanic practitioner and continues to teach creative empowerment classes.

I am rarely so excited about a book as I am about *Painting the Landscape of Your Soul*. I could just feel myself relax into a feeling of curiosity, awe, and wonder as I read this book. I know you will gain insight and healing as you read on and work with all the practices with Damini as your guide.

Enjoy the process, and be open to experiencing a joyful vitality returning to your life.

Sandra Ingerman
Santa Fe, New Mexico, July 2014

Foreword / Aviva Gold

I love free spontaneous painting. I love providing opportunities for others to paint in this way. Painting, fairy tales, movies, being in nature and creative play saved me as a child. As I grew and studied art professionally, the magic of free expression was lost. I watched children painting, envious and bereft for what I dearly missed. Then in midlife I was fortunate to rediscover the bliss of wild unselfconscious painting through which I fully experienced the empowerment and transformation I had for so long sought. I knew at once what I was meant to do with the rest of my life ... to facilitate others into the Source Paint adventure. In 1985 I was one of the pioneers in the spiritual Process Painting Movement. My book, *Painting From The Source* was published in 1998 and I have been fortunate to teach all over the world.

Now, in the midst of a mushrooming of Spiritual painting classes and books guiding folks in Creative Expression, this new book you are about to read, *Painting the Landscape of Your Soul*, is the latest unique bright star to join this much needed Heart Opening constellation.

In our current world of technology, urban living and gloomy news, we all still sense in our innermost being that there is mystery at the core of our existence. We yearn ever more fervently to connect with our roots, with nature and with the spiritual foundation of our beings.

Making art for me is a way of active prayer, a source of healing ... of refreshment and connection to the Divine Source of all creation. For me, and as you will read, for Damini Celebre, painting is a ritual of devotion which continually re-enchants our life and nourishes our soul. Painting is a path to deep self discovery.

After reading *Painting the Landscape of Your Soul*, painting with and personally interacting with Damini, I can clearly see that her life, teaching and book are a dynamic evolution toward wholeness and balance through creative expression. This book is replete with skillfully crafted tools, exercises, mindful rituals and ceremonies, from many Indigenous, Eastern and Western cultures. The book is a treasure trove of Damini's extensive knowledge, a definitive primer offered to discover the "Landscape of Your Soul" through painting ... No stone is left unturned for all levels of discovery and healing, for mind body and soul. You can feel Damini's love, experience, honesty and healing presence come through the pages.

Aviva Gold

Ojai, California, October 2014

Introduction / Chris Zydel

For a long time I was one of those people that Julia Cameron termed "shadow artists" in her book, *The Artist's Way*. I hung out with artists. I loved art. But I never thought I could actually make art. So I never tried.

I thought about maybe taking an art class, but I also have an allergy to following directions and being told what to do. But one day, one of my painter friends said to me, "You're the most visual person that I know. And there's a new kind of painting class where they don't tell you what to do. And you should probably go."

So I did.

This was my first experience of the intuitive painting process. And from the very first brush stroke I was in love. I could do whatever I wanted. There was no such thing as a mistake. Or even bad art. There was only painting. The world and myself in it just seemed incredibly alive.

I wasn't trying to become an artist. I just needed to do something that was creatively nurturing for me. But, as I continued to paint in this new and radical way, I discovered that this was so much more than just painting.

Through this process, I learned about the power of accepting whatever showed up. And learning to not see things as good or bad. I learned how to be curious instead of reactive to things like mess or ugliness.

At the time I was taking these classes, I was also in graduate school, getting a master's degree in clinical psychology. So the painting was a much needed respite from papers and deadlines, evaluations, and the stress of having to accomplish something. Painting also took me outside of my head. I wasn't thinking while I was painting. I was lost in a world of color and imagery and the sensuality of brush on paper.

And my life outside of the studio also started to change. As I listened to and trusted my intuition through the process of painting, I started listening to and trusting myself in other ways. I seemed to know more clearly how to proceed with my life. As I took more risks in my painting, I was willing to take more risks outside of the art studio.

I had faced the void so very many times in my painting, not knowing where the next stroke would lead me, but always trusting that something would happen if I just listened for the next instruction. I learned that going into what seemed like dark places always led to some sort of transformation, and I learned about the value of surrender to an energy greater than myself.

We are faced with the challenge and the opportunity to do things in ways that have never been done before. We can't entirely trust our minds (rationality and logic) to solve problems that our minds created. We can no longer remain separate from the Earth and our soul's desire. We can create what we want our new world to become. But, to take advantage of this opportunity, we need to activate different modes of perception. We need to embrace new ways of being and find passionate new voices of leadership and guidance.

Damini Celebre is one of those new voices. What she teaches us is not what we need to do but how we need to be in order to navigate through tumultuous changes and renew ourselves.

The ways of being that she articulates include the ancient Earth-based practices of shamanism and energy healing, the capacity to trust our intuitive knowing through art and the willingness to claim ourselves fully as creators and creative beings. These capacities or practices have lain fairly dormant and must be revitalized so we can make our way in this new world.

This reclamation is a journey into new and undiscovered lands and a journey back home. Damini lays the groundwork for understanding how to re-engage the lost parts of ourselves in ways that are clear, grounded, playful, and bursting with innovation

She is an artist of spirit and soul. This book is deeply informed by her artistic brilliance and her unshakable belief in the power of art to heal and allow us to grow into who we were meant to be. Damini masterfully takes us through the process of intuitive painting. Her message is one of joy and wonder. She teaches us how to see with our hearts, to be present in our bodies, and to become whole by dancing with color, shape, and form.

Painting the Landscape of Your Soul is filled with inspiration and powerfully transformational exercises that lead us on a pilgrimage into the miracle of our unique, essential selves. It supports us in discovering our own creative genius through paint on paper. And it also helps us identify and clear away anything (like our pesky inner critic) that blocks boundless creativity from flowing freely and blissfully as it was meant to.

It's not only a fabulous resource packed with useful information but an energy-healing experience that introduces creative techniques to transform us from the inside out.

We are ushered into a universe of creative blossoming and flourishing by a true medicine woman. The medicine that she so generously offers will not only heal our creative souls but heal the planet's soul. So dive into these pages with the enthusiasm with which they were so lovingly written, and allow yourself to be surprised and awestruck by what you can create when given the permission and blessing to do so.

The new world that waits to come into being will be grateful.

Preface: Being Creative

Creative energy is as vital as breathing. *Engaging your creative energy is healing.* Being creative brings joy, spontaneity, and carefreeness back into your life, so you can examine and remove limits you have put on yourself.

Embark on a journey that takes you through a process of *remembering, re-balancing,* and *realigning* YOU, so that you can be the authentic expression of the alive being you came here to be. *Painting the Landscape of Your Soul* allows your unconscious, intuitive muse to speak to you with paint on paper.

The explorations in this book will engage your creative muse so that you may explore your personal roadblocks, begin to change limiting self-beliefs, and bring into balance the many layers of your energetic being. You will experience a juicier, more alive, zesty you.

Creative healing starts from the outside, then moves deep inside. As healing, balance, and harmony shift your energetic fields into alignment to greater authenticity, *True*, then moves back to the outside. All the while, your creative healing realigns your energetic system and integrates your vitality, projecting your true self back out to the world.

This process is not about learning a new art technique, but the desire to live fully, the courage to listen deeply, and letting your creative muse guide you with color, shape, and form. The best thing about this is that no experience is necessary. Plus it's fun.

What makes *Painting the Landscape of Your Soul* unique is that it takes you on a healing journey using the creative process as the foundation for self-discovery and self-realization that invites your authentic self to emerge.

This book is a step-by-step journey of empowerment, engaging and re-awakening your innate creativity, learning to trust your intuitive voice, and reclaim your inner self with paint on paper. It incorporates deep, underlying principles of healing, such as energy medicine and shamanism.

If we want the world to be different we need to start with ourselves first.

My vision is that you go through the book once in the order the explorations are presented. The explorations take you through a healing process, a cycle. They will give you opportunities to get to know your true self, to remove beliefs that are not true to your soul. And once those imprints are removed, your energy will fill up with the trueness of you. Being filled up with your truth will allow you to feel stronger as you explore the rest of the healing process. You may repeat any exercise until you get the call to move to the next. After you go through the book once, you may feel called go back to some exercises, to explore deeper and deeper into the Landscape of Your Soul.

Our personal landscape

We all have a persona or facade that we present to the world. On the outside we tend to censor our thoughts and feelings, not necessarily showing all of ourselves to the world. Sometimes we don't even acknowledge all of who we are to ourselves; we push down events, thoughts, and ideas, even our dreams of who we are. Some of those hidden parts emerge right away when it is safe. We hide some parts of us in the shadow space to keep safe. Some parts get buried and forgotten completely.

The shadow space resides in our body and mind, where we tuck things away, like a closet. We hide parts of ourselves to keep them safe — parts of us that we feel don't fit within the world view around us. We unconsciously or consciously tuck them into the shadow space to retrieve another time. We also put away events, hurts, and arguments — even the more powerful parts of us can get put away because we don't feel safe sharing them, in that moment.

Putting parts of ourselves away for safety for a while, can be a useful practice. It's like cleaning your house and hiding old things that you don't want others to see in the closet. The problem occurs when we forget to take our old stuff out again. The closet is only so big, and eventually it fills up. This is when symptoms start to appear. Symptoms can manifest as belly pain, depression, sleeplessness, or chronic shoulder pain. They are signs that your body wants you to look in your shadow space, start to clean it out, and bring into the light all aspects of yourself.

What lives in our shadow space doesn't change, or get better, or heal itself. Rather, parts of ourselves that we put away go into a holding pattern, get dusty, and stagnate. The only way to create more space in yourself is to peek into your shadow space, notice, honor, and heal those parts of yourself. This happens by shining a little light on them and allowing your shadow story to come out via your unconscious muse. Let your shadow parts speak to you with color, shape, and form. Expressing your shadow parts frees up your energetic systems in your *bodymindspirit*, bringing vitality and healing to your soul. Bringing full aliveness and healing to your soul, my friends, is what the intuitive creative self *does best*.

Our intuitive self knows how to bring these shadow parts into the light and heal them. This is not art therapy. This is your *bodymindspirit's* natural ability to self-regulate, rebalance, rekindle, and remember all of who you are.

The intuitive self is intelligent, in that it only brings as many little bits of information up as you are able to understand, remember, and integrate. How? By using our first language: color, shape, and form. (Sound is also one of our first means of expression. So for all musicians and dancers out there, you may be more inclined to interact with your creative self through sound, rhythm, and movement.)

The inner landscape of your soul is vast with many landscapes, emotions, ideas and experiences—created by you and the Divine. Imagine shining a little light on your shadow space to revitalize your inner landscape and start manifesting your dreams in the world.

This creative process allows you to look deeply within and enliven your creative life force—with many methods, including painting, writing, moving, making music, collaging, singing, filming, photographing, and acting, to name a few. Are you ready to meet the authentic you?

The purpose of art is washing the dust
of daily life off our souls.

—Pablo Picasso

Roots and Bones

Do what you love. Know your own bone;
gnaw at it, bury it, unearth it,
and gnaw it still.

— Thoreau

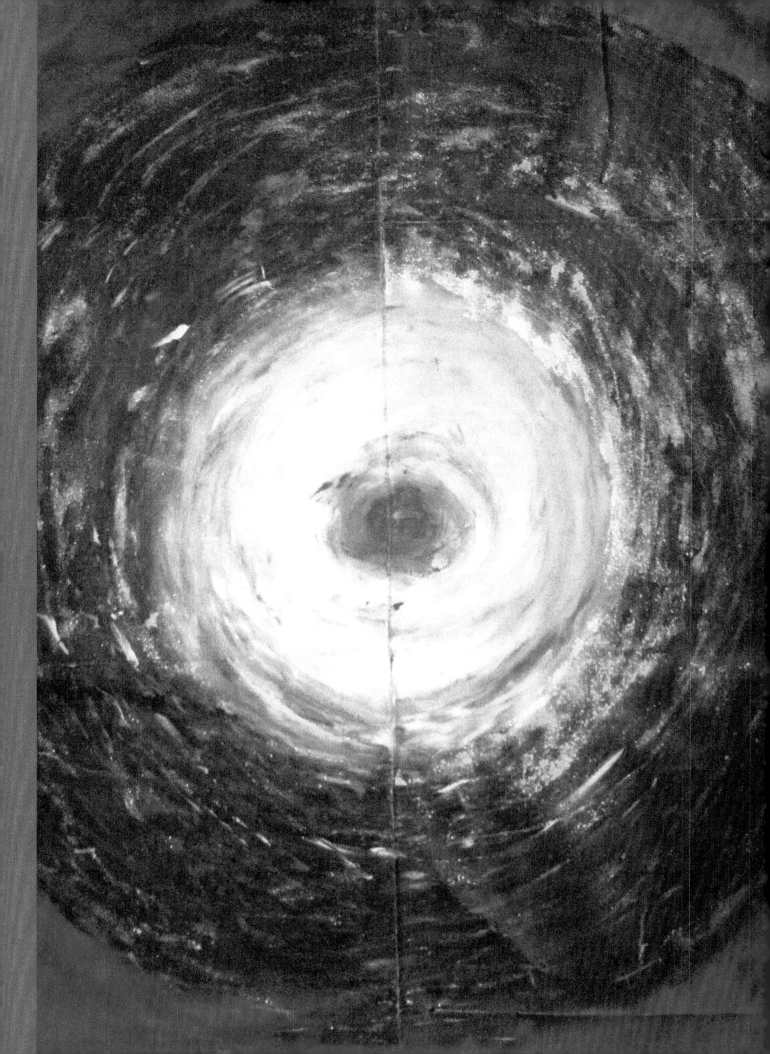

The Power of the Creative Spirit

What makes the creative process so important? What makes a person choose to explore their creative instincts (or do I say life?), no matter where they lead?

I always wanted to be an artist. My family is Italian-American, which means hardworking folks with no airy-fairy dreams of being artists. My mom's *hobby* was painting. Her grandfather painted religious icons and murals in churches throughout Italy. I never could paint like them — so I wondered if I had the talent to be an artist.

My whole life, I have loved to make art and in my heart always considered myself an artist. As an adult, I taught at prestigious art schools, and my artwork was shown around the world. I thought I was on my way. I applied for a grant offered to fine artists, and when I didn't receive it, I asked for feedback from the judges (so I might learn from my *mistakes*). Their feedback was extremely harsh. I took the rejection personally and slowly started to shut down my creativity. I changed careers. Over time, I stopped creating altogether and became depressed, lethargic, and sluggish (in my *bodymind-spirit*). I didn't even want to do anything creative because it hurt so badly. I didn't want to feel the *pain*. I took in other peoples' good/

bad judgments and let my love for the creative act get repressed, get tucked away.

I created art because that was the only thing I could do that made me feel alive. Searching for something else to bring aliveness to me, I directed all my energy to the healing arts and stuffed any creative urge deep down within myself into the shadow space. I found a quote at that time that said healing and creativity are the same energy. I consoled myself with that quote for years.

I channeled my creative life force into learning many healing modalities, including Asian bodywork, acupuncture, and shamanism. Over time, I started to have creative bursts. Images came into my mind, and I would have to draw them at that moment while the energy was there, or the images would go away. My creative intuition was trying to get me to come back home, back to myself. I was extremely private about my drawings, not wanting to show them to anyone for fear my creative moments would go away, or I would be criticized. I was still squashing my creative expression into a little box, little safe moments in time, allowing myself to hide and be small.

Deep in my soul I wanted to create again. My intuitive self brought me to shamanism to allow my heart to heal, to feel the Spirit That Lives In All Things around me and inside me so I might have the courage to be who I am. That took years, and one day in a journey I was told to "Paint with the heart." I was very good at taking orders — then.

By the time I got to my first intuitive painting class, I was shut down, tiny, invisible, and feeling left out. After that first class, I had a

glimmer of *me*, and I welcomed myself back home. I know that being creative is the only thing that ever mattered to me. Being creative is how I feel most alive. When I have walked away from my creativity, I have felt like I died a slow death until I came back to my creative spirit.

When you start living only partially, it's hard to notice at first. Think about when you get a chest cold, and you start shallow breathing. Somehow your body/mind convinces itself that this is the way you will be for the rest of your life. True, you are living and breathing, but are you *alive*? For me, being in my creative flow is as vital as breathing. I often joke that I need to create, or I will die. It's that simple (for me). What about you? Yes, you can ignore your creative spirit, but you will live only part of your greatness and beauty.

I was never one to create on demand. It always had to be when the inspiration filled me. Laughing, I'd say I had creative Tourette's Syndrome. An idea would pop into my head, and I would have to draw/paint/write it down immediately before the creative impulse was gone. The closest I came to on-demand creating was when I did Zen brushwork, and even then I would spend hours finding that quiet place inside me. Then, if I was lucky, inspiration would come, and a mark would come forth. I cannot force myself to make art — which is not good for someone who wanted to do this for a living.

In 2006, Aviva Gold's book, *Painting from the Source,* found its way into my hands. I never considered asking Source to create with me. I slowly started to reconnect to my creative expression and more

importantly, to accessing Source inside me. That understanding perco-
lated within me for a few more years until I received the invitation.

The invitation ... In 2008, at a shamanic retreat at the Ghost Ranch in
Abiquiú, New Mexico, I got an order from the Universe, my higher self,
God/Goddess urging me to: *Do painting from the heart.*

The next morning, I was excitedly telling someone about my order as I picked up a name tag from the floor that someone had left behind from another class. The class name was "Painting from Your Wild Heart." Who knew such a class existed?

Retreat … Six months later, I went to California for the Wild Heart painting retreat. That first night everyone walked into the studio and started painting right away. I looked around, confused. Chris Zydel, the facilitator, asked, "What's wrong?"

"What's our intention? How do we start?" I asked her. She told me to start painting and see what my intuitive self brings forth. Incredulous, I said, "Is that it?"

She laughed and said, "Yes, Damini, that's what you traveled 3,000 miles for!"

Coming home… Her words provided me with a much-longed-for invitation: To come back to my creative self — to feel alive — to bring to the forefront what was nearest to my heart. And I did!

Epiphany … Then something unexpected and amazing happened. As I dove deeper into a dialogue with my inner creative muse, *my intuitive self merged with my healer self.* The result was life changing. I noticed that painting class participants had the same, powerful healing experience as my patients. A powerful healing matrix aligned, rebalanced, and started healing from the inside out, all by bringing paint to paper and speaking the language of color, shape, and form.

Join me on a healing journey back to yourself — back to the part of you that feels most alive.

We are all creative beings

We are all creative beings and creativity is our birthright. Just like breathing and our hearts beating. We all have the gift to express ourselves with color, shape, and form (if we stop judging and criticizing ourselves). Creativity manifests in your life in a variety of ways: when you are trying to figure out how to handle a situation, what clothes to wear, or even what to cook for dinner. When I talk about creativity, I am not talking about being an artist, which is a profession that requires talent, propensity, training, and skill.

Luckily we are all born creative. Accessing your creative self is as easy as breathing (with a little coaxing). Call back your inner four-year-old, and remember the joy and excitement when you were given crayons, rattles, paint, and paper. Remember a time before you had to be good at something, a time before inhibitions. Engaging your creative life force will allow you to stay alive and thrive.

In this book, I invite you to use kid's paint and paper, because it's inexpensive and freeing. Kid's paint will help to wake up your fearless four-year-old, who doesn't need any instructions, just goes for it, and doesn't worry about lines or any other constraints.

I invite you to explore your inner landscape with that same freedom and joy as your four-year-old: Explore, smear, and draw, using brushes, fingers, and toes. This is your creative birthright. Allow the joy, innocence and freedom of exploration you had as a child to come out and play, with no restrictions, time limits, or should-haves.

Setting the 'scape

Intuition... inner wisdom...

I'll use the word *intuition* a lot in this book. I am referring to our sixth sense—our inner wisdom that we experience via our senses: clairsentience (feeling/ touching), clairaudience (hearing/listening), clairalience (smelling), claircognizance (knowing). You use your intuition every day when you make choices that feel right to you. I'll use the word *feel* to include all of the ways you sense something. When you are faced with two choices and one feels better to you, that is your intuition communicating with you. Your intuition is not a mental/mind choice but an instinctual body/gut/feeling.

Body scan

Here's an exercise to help you get a sense of what is true and right, a YES for you:

- Relax, sit comfortably, and close your eyes.

- Scan your body — use your mind to do a quick survey of how your body feels. Start at your forehead, top of your head, back of your head, shoulders, chest, heart area, belly, back, thighs, knees, calves, ankles, and feet. Notice which areas are tight, relaxed, hot, cold, calling for attention, or wanting no attention focused on them.

- Then say to yourself, "My name is (state your name)." Do a quick body scan and register how you feel.

- Then say to yourself, "My name is _____." (If you're a woman, say a male name. If you're a man, say a woman's name.) Again, do a quick body scan and register how you feel.

They will feel different. One may feel contracted; the other may feel expanded. The sensation that you feel when you speak your true name is a YES. The other is a definite NO.

We use our body feelings every day; we just don't realize it. For instance, if you are walking down the street and turn the corner you get a NO if it doesn't feel right or doesn't feel safe. This is your body — intuition speaking — your gut sense.

Intuition is experienced as a quick understanding that comes from a gut feeling response; it is not controlled by your rational thinking mind.

For the sake of this book and the intuitive creative process, let's also refer to your intuitive self as your inner child, wise one, muse, and your heart. You will access your wise, all-knowing, creative self directly and sometimes you will bring your awareness to your body; both will give you feedback during the creative process about color, shape, and form and where to place it.

Seeing with the heart: a shamanic view

Another part of our landscape is the world around us, the Web of Life, where everything around us is alive and has spirit. There is a phrase, *As above, so below; As within, so without.* Meaning we are not separated from the world around us — we are part of it.

Anthropologists study people and their habitats, and describe indigenous cultures filled with people who *see with the heart*, also called *shamans*. The root of all indigenous cultures (yours and mine) is a deep connection to the world surrounding them, the Web of Life, which includes: Earth, Air, Water, Fire, Animal, Bird, Rock; our ancestors, descendants; our helping and guardian spirits. These are our connection with the invisible and magical world around us.

Part of reclaiming all the parts of ourselves is to regain our connection with the Web of Life. We will use our intuitive creative self as the intermediary between ordinary reality (our day-to-day stuff) and non-ordinary reality (the invisible realms of life all around us).

Seeing with the heart, shamanism, is about relationships. What is a relationship? Simply put, it's an exchange of energy — seeing the truth of everything around us (and within us). It all influences who we are and our place in this world.

A shaman is a man or woman who uses the ability to see "with the strong eye" or "with the heart" to travel into hidden realms. The shaman interacts directly with the spirits to address the spiritual aspect of illness and perform soul retrievals, retrieve lost power, as well as remove spiritual blockages. The shaman also divines healers, doctors, priests and priestesses, psychotherapists, mystics, and storytellers.

Shamanism is the most ancient spiritual practice known to humankind. Some anthropologists believe that the practice dates back over 100,000 years. The word "shaman" comes from the Tungus tribe in Siberia and it means spiritual healer or one who sees in the dark. Shamanism has been practiced in Siberia, Asia, Europe, Africa, Australia, Greenland, and native North and South America.

— Sandra Ingerman

We are in relationship with the critters, trees, grass, and rock — the Elements around us. Once we realize everything around us is alive and has spirit, our relationships build. (*As within, so without.*)

Our inner landscape is composed of both ordinary and nonordinary worlds. There is ordinary reality: your life, your job, what you can see with your eyes, hear with your ears. Then there is nonordinary reality: the world your can feel with your *heart* and your senses. This world is where you can have direct revelations with your helping spirits, who guide you and teach you from a higher perspective. (They are not confined to the world of the body or physical plane).

Your heart holds the *truth* of who you are. Your intuitive self directly communicates with your heart; color, shape, and form is the language of your heart and your intuitive self.

In this book, we will be listening, dialoguing, and building relationships with your creative self, your compassionate helping spirits, and your intuitive self — all living in your heart. Each of these parts shares a different perspective of you. These parts call forth memories, stories, and learnings. They reveal your blocks, so you may heal them and live a fully authentic life.

Calling forth, seeking guidance and healing from your intuitive, creative self and the Web of Life is powerful and life changing.

As we move through this book, let's remember that we are in relationship with all that surrounds us. I invite you to look to the natural world for guidance and insight as you explore your creativity.

Once you remember that we are all connected, watch for those synchronistic moments of connection with the Web of Life. If you learn something about yourself while painting, you will notice that same learning (or understanding) will show up in your day-to-day life.

Energy and time are not linear. Sometimes the Web of Life will give you clues, answers about what you are searching for before the question arises in your mind. How many times have you picked up the phone to call someone and they are already on the line? Have you been out in nature and thought about a particular bird then heard its call? Have you tried to decide between two choices and something odd happens to get your attention: a hawk flies in front of you, or your phone rings, or something falls off the wall? (*As within, so without.*) We are truly connected with the Web of Life. It's time for us to remember!

A STORY
Dragonfly message

I was traveling to a painting retreat and had been thinking about my intention for the week, a starting place for my painting. Walking outside the airport terminal, I looked down and saw a big blue dragonfly in the street next to the curb. I bent down to move it out of the street and realized it was dead. It was irides-cent blue and perfect. I picked it up and took it with me — my mascot for the week, my messenger/omen of seeing all pos-sibilities for transformation. Dragonflies have sixteen sets of eyes, a reminder to see my life from many different viewpoints. And possibilities and transformation did show up. My painting showed me, in layers of paint, how I need to trust who I am, my voice, and my heart and paint out my limiting belief of not being good enough. That limiting belief was keeping me from being my big, bright, beautiful self.

The Web of Life all around us speaks to us as clearly and as deeply as our intuitive self and our helping spirits do. We just need to listen.

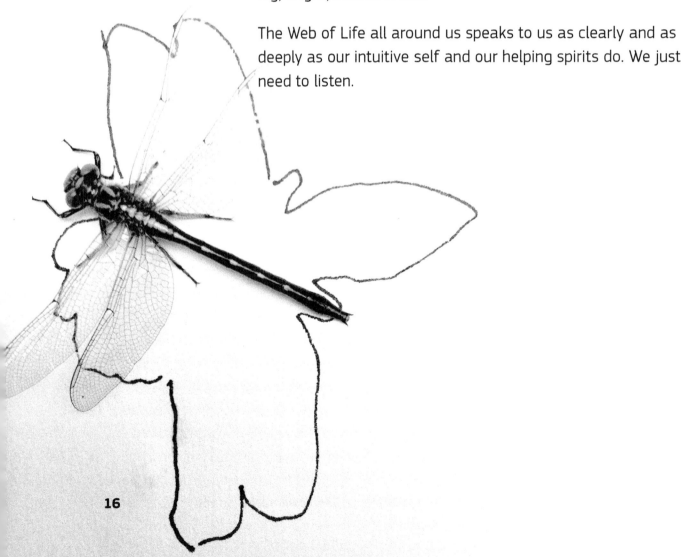

All spiritual traditions teach that everything
manifests on a spiritual level before manifesting
on the physical. Where we have power right now
to create change on the planet is by incorporating
spiritual practices into our lives.

—Sandra Ingerman

Our first language

I joked with my friends that English is not my first language and about how hard it is to write and speak in groups. My fear and worry that I might use grammatically awkward words and be judged as *stupid* would often paralyze me.

When I told them that my first language was color, shape, and form, it dawned on me: This is the first language for *all* of us. Colorful shapes were dangled above our cribs. Our preverbal toys were red, yellow, blue, and green. They were balls, squares, and triangles — *color, shape, and form.* Some of us moved over to written language, to best communicate our thoughts, desires, and wishes. For many of us, our language of color, shape, and form is the easiest, most natural way to express ourselves. Our first language connects us with our intuitive creative self. A picture speaks a thousand words. Yes, our creative self speaks volumes through color, shape, and form.

What makes the intuitive painting process so powerful is that you can plug into that creative, preverbal part of yourself — that part of you that knows the freedom of expression, your true voice, and the aliveness and joy that comes with creative expression.

Invite your inner child/adult/woman/man (oh hell — let's just say that big, bright, shiny, colorful, visually articulate, excited, contemplative, sober, sad, silly self) to come out and play, have fun, and make a mess. Splash paint, paint rainbows, finger paint with red, bright pink, or black, just because it feels good and gives you a sense of freedom that you don't get in your day-to-day life. Allow all that follows to come forth!

I found I could say things with color and shapes that I couldn't say any other way—things I had no words for.

—Georgia O' Keeffe

Color, shape, and form articulate whatever needs to be expressed via your inner self without judgment, criticism, or should-haves. Creative expression gives you a deeper, truer experience of freedom and energy that you then take out into the world.

Energy!?

What comes to your mind when you hear the word *energy*? Movement, electricity, the hum of your refrigerator, the sun's light rays, movement as you dance? We have our bones, nervous system, and vascular system in our bodies. We also have systems in our bodies that are unseen, but absolutely felt, called the *subtle energy systems*: our chakras (vortices of energy) as described in ancient India; meridians (rivers of energy), as described in ancient Asia. These energy systems generate the movement of our bodies, inspire our minds, and excite our senses. We say it all the time, "I am full of energy," or, "I am drained of energy." Yes, we can talk about good nutrition, chemistry, and vitamins, but there are more ways to engage and replenish our energy. We get energy from good conversation, being out in nature—and doing what we love. When our hearts are full, and we are enjoying ourselves, we are thriving, not just surviving. Using all of our senses and life force keeps us moving and engaged in life.

So what does this all have to do with the creative process? We know now that our creative energy is a birthright, just like breathing. Unfortunately, when we get stressed and too busy, we lapse into survival mode — allocating only enough energy for what must be done. If we stay in survival mode, we are hypervigilant, which wears us out. We lose energy and focus. Very slowly the twinkle in our eyes (which reflects our spirit) starts to grow dim, indicating that we are losing vitality. As we start to lose energy, our breathing becomes shallow; we move slower, and then we begin to get sick and manifest illness, such as insomnia, confusion, depression, or body aches.

We can get an energy infusion by tapping into our creativity. When you are being creative, your eyes brighten; your heart lightens, and the sides of your mouth rise into a smile; you are having fun and doing what feels right for you and for that moment. Your *bodymindspirit* muscle memory is full of vitality and lightheartedness. Your hopes and dreams get awakened.

There are many different ways I will use the word *energy* in this book. We have established that subtle energy moves through our body — it cannot be seen, but is felt. This subtle energy can be fueled by good nutrition, movement, and doing what we love and infuses vitality into our *body-mind-soul-spirit*.

There is also feel-good energy when you do something that is fun or exciting — for instance, painting with yellow, playing a good groove, singing, or dancing.

Energy motivates you, excites you, energizes you to move forward with an idea or thought. Energy wakes you up and brings aliveness back to your life. On the flip side, strongly avoiding an idea or situation, aka resistance, has energy to it as well. Energy does not have *good* or *bad* associations.

Mystics talk about energy as the vibration that forms the world. It can be the spiritual life force that moves through all living beings. It can be an exchange of force between two things, like how atoms attract or repel each other. Other names for energy are: Chi, Ki, Parana, Shakti, Great Spirit, Holy Spirit, Ashe, Mana.

The Asian character for energy, Qi (chee) is described as the movement and force of steam as it rises from boiling water, which is invisible, always in motion, and life giving. A simple way to understand energy is to ask yourself how you feel when you are full of energy or when you are not. Notice how both questions make your body and mind feel. Store that feeling in your body/mind memory, to use as a guide as you paint the Landscape of Your Soul.

The power of color

When we are born, we don't see in color. In fact, our vision doesn't even start to develop until after we are born. At first we see only black, white, and gray. As we begin to develop our color vision, we see only bold shapes and patterns of colors. After about four months, we start to see full color, full shapes, and patterns. We start to explore sound and texture at six months, then starting at nine months, we explore spatial relationships: sorting, stacking, and arranging.

When infant eyes absorb a world of virgin visions, colors are processed purely, in pre-linguistic parts of the brain. As adults, colors are processed in the brain's language centers, refracted by the concepts we have for them.

—Brandon Keim, "Babies See Pure Color, but Adults Peer Through Prism of Language" in *Wired*

The power of color stirs our subconscious in ways we don't always understand at first. When we are young, we respond to color with a pure gut response (belly brain); it is not until we are adults that our reactions get filtered through our mind and then we *know* what we are feeling. Recently, there have been a lot of articles written about the belly brain, which processes all emotional experiences through the belly first, then routes them up to the mind, which labels them. When we encounter something that is emotionally charged, we often can't voice it at first, but we can begin to understand it when we notice where we feel it in our bodies.

Ahh, but let's go back to our responses to color: As we grow up we learn the psychological associations of color. For example, red is hot and active — blue is cool and calm.

In color psychology, there are all kinds of associations with colors. There are associations related to the energy centers of our body: the meridians, the chakras, even the Elements. Specific colors are used for public buildings because of their emotional associations. Do you remember the color of your grade school hallway and classrooms? Chances are they were chosen to either stimulate you or calm you down. Feelings also have colors associated with them. Often they are culturally specific. What black means in the United States is very different from its meaning in Asia. Let's not get attached to what these meanings are because once you put a name on something, you stop exploring it. Allow your gut — your intuitive self — to choose colors when painting. One color, one mark, one color, one mark.

Color is light and light is energy. Scientists have found that actual physiological changes take place in human beings when they are exposed to certain colors. Colors can stimulate, excite, depress, tranquilize, increase appetite and create a feeling of warmth or coolness. This is known as chromo dynamics.

— Speider Schneider, *The Psychology Of Color In Design*

Roots

Spontaneous intuitive creative work focuses on personal empowerment through self-discovery and was most likely derived from art therapy techniques. Art therapy is a medical-based system, looking for what and when something was broken, and its aim is to mend that wound. By contrast, the intuitive creative process is based on discovering your true self, your inner voice that allows your heart to open and enliven your life.

Personal exploration creation focuses on the here and now; and the growth that moves from the present forward. Traditional therapy looks at the past and how you got here.

Intuitive-based creation also has roots in the Surrealist movement with *pure psychic automatism* (automatic drawing) and the spiritual art movement of the early 1900s. Both movements combined intuition, exploration, and spirituality, which is the core of intuitive based creative expression.

The artist must train not only his eye, but his soul. The artist must have something to say. Mastery over form is not his goal but Adaption of form to its inner meaning.

—Kandinsky, *Concerning the Spiritual in Art*

A Brief History of intuitive painting

Here are a few leaders in the world of creativity for self-discovery.
Each of them has taken this work in a different direction.

- 1989, Betty Edwards, *Drawing on the Right Side of the Brain.*

- 1992, Shaun McNiff, a pioneer in Expressive Arts Therapy
  and author of *Art as Medicine.*

- 1992, Julia Cameron, *The Artist Way: a spiritual path to
  higher creativity.*

- 1995, Pat Allen, *Art as Way of Knowing,*

- 1996, Michelle Cassou and Stewart Cubley, co-authored
  Life Paint Passion.

- 1998, Aviva Gold, *Painting from the Source.*

*No Experience necessary ... Intuitive creation
is a form of expression that everyone can do.
You don't need to know how to draw a straight
line or hold a paintbrush. It's about focusing on
personal explorations to discover who you are,
exploring your blind spots and little by little,
acknowledging your authentic self.*

Getting to know you ...
getting to know
all the little things
about you ...

— The King and I

All about You

Get what you need to grow. Humans and plants grow in surprisingly similar ways. In the spring, we both experience growth. We move from the darkness of winter (unconsciousness), feel the sap rise deep inside us (the desire for self-growth), and reach toward the light of the sun (expansion/enlightenment).

Plants do it. So do we.

We are all aware of those tender shoots rising from the earth. The bud forms, the bloom opens, and then that bloom tracks the sun. Underground, or unconsciously, the roots weave and intertwine, and grow deep and wide. They constantly reach toward nutrients that will bring growth (in our case, personal growth and change).

You are doing this right now by reading this book, and so is anyone who is searching for deeper meaning in their life.

Your true self is willing to take the underground journey to discover whatever it needs to evolve. What your roots reach for will change with each cycle of growth. You require different nutrients as you grow and change.

The bloom, that is you, will keep following the sun. You will go through many little deaths, rebirths, blooms, and reblooms once you are on the path of self-discovery.

Let's grow and bloom!

Body

What do we know about our bodies? We know our bodies are more than machines with computers guiding them. We are more than tissue, bones, and fluid. Our bodies are exquisite carriers for our souls to have a life experience. What we choose to do with our bodies is up to us. We can look at parts of our bodies and know that our hands grasp, our legs propel us, our feet balance us, and eyes allow us to see. But what makes us more than robots is that our senses and emotions allow us to feel the environment around us, and we have cognitive capacity that allows us to make associations, to mature, and to develop. In Western (or allopathic) medicine, our body functions are divided into sections: physical medicine, mental medicine, pediatrics (or kids' medicine), and hormonal medicine, to name a few. The body is so vast that it needs to be divided into parts to learn about it — to know how it functions, as well as how to fix it.

When I talk about our bodies in this book, I am referring to the wonderful vessel that holds our soul-spirit so that we may experience life and the feeling of being alive.

I see our bodies as whole, harmonious, interconnected systems. I don't look to fix but to realign and balance our systems.

In Eastern (holistic) medicine, the focus expands to consider the connection between our bodies and our emotions. We understand that if we get anxious, we will feel our hearts beating faster, our chest will

> Awareness of the body-mind connection is **essential** to unite creativity and healing.

constrict or we will not be able to focus on a task. Watching for subtle body signals (skin crawling, sore lower back, funny tummy, restlessness) allows us to recognize that something is out of harmony in our body-emotion connection.

We use the language of metaphor to speak about things that are invisible, abstract, and intangible, such as feelings, sensations, and our unconscious.

Once you recognize this body-emotion connection, you might notice that different body parts are talking to you. I invite you to feel what your body has to say. Do not take on associations that you heard when growing up or that others have written about. One of the goals of this book is that you identify and *own* what you feel, what you know to be true. Don't get lost in what other authorities tell you. Trust your body to lead the way. In the creative process, what is most important is that you allow whatever images come up — and whatever feelings come up. Let your body and feelings communicate with you *without judgment.* Allow them to arise and don't try to interpret. Then ask what color, shape, or form your feelings bring forth.

Feelings

What are feelings and emotions? Feelings are feedback from your senses. They are sensations that you experience in your body. Emotions are reactions and expressions of *feelings*.

You may be thinking at this point ... feelings ... *feelings*. I thought we were talking about creativity — now we are talking about feelings. What does this have to do with the creative process? This book will take you on a journey through your inner landscape to discover parts of yourself (feelings, beliefs, dreams) that you have put away. As you integrate all of your *landscapes*, you can walk in the world a whole, strong person. Focusing on both your body and feelings allows you to paint from a place of feeling and intuition, not from your clever mind.

Our bodies use color, shape, and form to translate what we feel, using our body-mind sensations to explore our deep truths. If we depend on our minds and the stories we *think* we know about ourselves, there would be little room and desire for self-discovery and growth. Our minds divert us from the present moment by telling a story of something that happened in the past and/or what will happen in the future. Working with feelings in our bodies keeps us in the *present moment* — one breath — one mark — one moment toward knowing our whole true selves.

Sometimes feelings/emotions pop up so quickly that they are gone in a flash, and our minds don't even register them. Sometimes body sensation shows up before the mind registers that something is off kilter. Sometimes a feeling shows up not just as a body ache, but as feeling disagreeable, tired, or hungry because of bumping into something

that rose up from our unconscious, possibly even from our preverbal days — so we don't even have words to describe it. But we do have color, shape, and form to keep it moving.

It's important to note that when you invite your creative self to come forth, explore, and express itself, some of your stuck feelings may get released as that creative energy starts to move.

What do you do with the emotions that show up? In this creative process, all emotions are okay; do not judge them or hold them in. Don't let your emotions take over your experiences and force you to act out. Simply acknowledge them. When you recognize a feeling or emotion, ask how it wants to be expressed with color, shape, form, sound, movement. Do not run from that emotion — instead, let your emotions and your body move the energy until it has shifted or run its course. Feelings and emotions are part of being alive. Following the energy of the present moment is your point of *greatest aliveness* — right now, right here, in this breath — this moment. There is no need to attach a story to that feeling or emotion. Let the feelings come and go, like your breath.

We human beings are vast, exquisite, and carry the light of the Divine in our hearts. Therefore, we need systems, stories, archetypes, and metaphor to organize and make sense of us.

Core Emotions: Core emotions are pure expressions of the heart. In Asian medicine, it is said that the heart is a vessel where all feelings pass though, and it warns us: if emotions get stuck, they create illness.

Pure emotions of joy, empathy, fear, grief, and hope come and go. They get expressed and then move on. If they get stuck in the vessel — whether that is in the heart or another part of the body — they become the embodiment of the emotion: sadness, worry, terror, anger, pensiveness, shock, surprise, hate, desire, fright, or exhaustion. There are *core emotions* and *reactions*.

Core emotions can be expressed through facial reactions and are driven by the limbic system of the brain (that reptilian part of us that doesn't censor, just expresses). Core emotions are love, gratitude, happiness, peacefulness, hope, joy, humility, fear.

These eight core emotions can be felt by any animal and human. Each core emotion has three components: First, physical arousal occurs. Second, there are thoughts about an emotion. Third, there are behaviors, or what we do with the emotion.

Reactions: Reactions are emotional responses to stimuli, but not core basic hormonal body responses.

Here are a few examples of emotional reactions: acceptance, anger, anticipation, curiosity, contempt, courage, disgust, fright, grief, guilt, loneliness, lust, pride, sadness, shame, and surprise.

Gut feelings, which are visceral responses to someone or something, originate in the belly or gut first, and then travel up to the brain/mind to be labeled.

Nonverbal conversation with your body

Let's see if you can get in touch with what you're feeling and where you feel it. Close your eyes and notice any body part that is subtly or not so subtly vying for your attention. When you encounter a place that is whispering or screaming to you, ask it to express itself in color, shape, form, sound, and movement. Don't censor it. Listen to the first impression that comes. Just be aware. Notice if there is an emotion attached to that area. Just be aware of how your body feels and how it wants to express that feeling.

Emotion: an often conscious hormonal body-mind biological response to a situation.

Feeling: a reaction to a situation that starts in the gut, often unconscious at first, until it travels to the brain for a label.

Gut reaction: instinctual visceral emotional reaction to a situation.

CREATE

MOVE IT

Grab some crayons (or a musical instrument, or move your body), and choose one of the emotions on the core emotion list, look at the word and, without getting your mind involved too much, notice where you feel it in your body.

- Let that body part direct your expression with the crayon.

- Don't judge it. Don't try to put a story to it.

- Be present with the emotion, and express your feelings that arise at this very moment.

Subtle body energy

The viewpoint of this book is holistic. In the holistic view there is no separation between the *bodymindspirit*. All parts of us interact and respond together, and we need harmony in all of our parts to be healthy and whole. There are body, mind, and spirit associations for different parts of the body, and there are also various metaphors and understandings about the energetic systems of the body.

General terms of understanding:

Body: Chakra, meridians, nerve plexus, organs, bones, muscles, cells.

Mind: Carl Jung's work in understanding the mind/psychology through the use of archetypes. Cellular memory, body memory.

Spirit: A force of something greater than ourselves. I sometimes refer to this force as the Divine, Universe, Goddess, God, Supreme Being, All That Is, Spirit ... please feel free to use your own reference to Spirit.

The subtle energy systems of the body give the physical body life force and have a direct response on balancing and healing mind and spirit. These systems of the body can't be seen with modern technology (x-rays, CAT scans, etc.), but you can sense them.

The three major subtle body-healing systems we will discuss throughout this book are: the auric bodies, the chakra system, and the Asian system of energy channels in the body called meridians. Both chakras and acupoints are access zones connecting to a larger series of pathways that move life force through the body.

The auric bodies: Auric energy is an electromagnetic energy field that emanates from the physical body in several layers, starting at skin level and expanding out beyond the body. This energy field turns into energy vortexes, Chakras.

Chakras: Chakras are energy vortexes in the core midline of our bodies. Chakras are like hubs of energy moving in a clockwise direction and are about the size of your fist. Like any organic energy, they vary according to how you feel. If you feel expansive, chances are your chakra size is normal to big. If you feel small or inward, chances are that your chakras are smaller. Chakras have color associations but because the chakra system comes from Mother India, it is a very old system with many different traditions. The associations tend to shift a little with various traditions, but the spirit of each chakra remains the same. There are commonly seven major chakras recognized.

Asian medicine: Originating from Japan, China, and Korea, this system of medicine shares an important concept for the intuitive creator: The concept of microcosm and macrocosm, which means, what we feel inside us is reflected around us. Asian medicine also has a metaphorical system of understanding the body that helps us express deep understanding of complex concepts with images and stories. Here is a great example of how metaphor can tell you a complex story about how your energy came into form.

One of the first questions posed in Asian medicine is: "How does energy become matter or body?" Lao Tzu in the *Tao Te Ching* answers "The One becomes two. The two becomes three. The three becomes 10,000 things." The Great One becomes heaven (energy) and earth

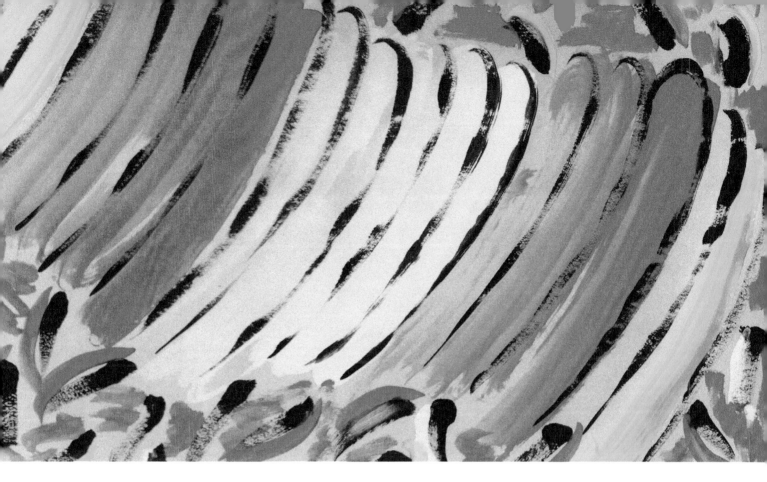

(flesh/bones/energy). Then heaven and earth energies create human (blood/flesh). Then the 10,000 things (everything) is born.

We humans stand between heaven and earth, receiving the gifts of being embodied and the gifts of being infused with life force/spirit.

The auric layers and chakras vitalize parts of our body, mind, and spirit. They draw, store, and distribute energy up from the earth to the heavens and from the heaven to the earth, meeting in the middle — the Heart. The meridians spread that energy from the chakras throughout our body, mind, and spirit, filling us with vitality. So when we see, hear, smell, touch, and create, we commingle the infusion of earth and heaven within our hearts, and share it with the world ... the 10,000 things!

Divine energy is regulated in the body, through the subtle bodies. The subtle bodies interact with the world around us. We are part of the 10,000 things *(As within, so without)*.

The meridian system consists of channels of invisible energy lines in the body that start from a major organ and then spread out in the body, flowing up or down, from earth or heaven energy. This is how your subtle body energy comes into form. Meridians are named for their organ of origin such as heart, liver, or kidney. We can also speak of the expression or archetype of a meridian in terms such as *visionary, one who embraces, the inspirer,* and *the creator.*

Each of these three systems of energetic medicine (auric, chakras, and meridians) has a special quality about it that makes it ideal to discuss in a metaphorical, healing, creative process.

There are many systems and diverse ways to categorize our personalites or to explain what we are feeling. Other ways to observe energy movement in the body are:

- Balance of top and bottom (vertical energy)

- Side to side (horizontal energy)

- Front to back, or one side to the opposite side (diagonal energy)

We will explore these systems more deeply as we go through the explorations, but for now I want to provide the necessary foundation for understanding. Let's think about the major energy systems in our bodies as: auras, chakras, meridians, and Heaven and Earth energy.

All these layers of our subtle body systems bring expression, meaning, metaphor, and aliveness to us. When you bring your intention, imagination, and love for your self-expression and combine it with your subtle energy systems, *healing happens*.

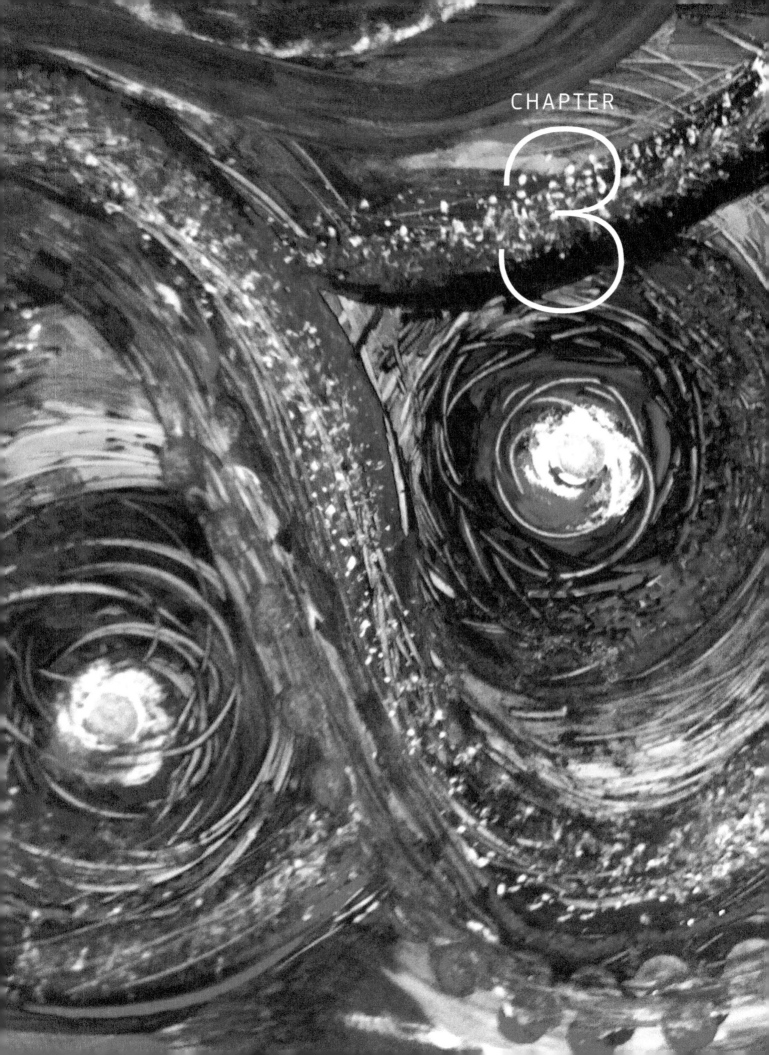

CHAPTER

3

Intuitive Creation

Learned skills — like math, cooking, painting, or music — depend on mind and muscle memory. When we create from an intuitive place; we do not respond from a learned muscle memory in our minds. We respond from our bellies, our guts, and our hearts. When I invite you to paint from your heart and your gut, I am asking you to listen; listen deeply to the sublime place inside of you, and respond to any feeling that arises.

Spirit: Painting from the heart

Our heart, a big muscle the size of a fist, resides in the center of our chest. It is that blood-pumping, oxygen-moving, life-producing organ that keeps us alive. Yet, our emotional heart also has to do with our feelings: Love, joy, heartache, sadness, elation, infatuation. This heart is the vessel of the Spirit, the house of feelings, all governed by the heart chakra, which circulates and tends those feelings throughout our *bodymindspirit*.

The heart's archetype is the sovereign queen or king, a benevolent ruler who cares deeply for all that happens in the queen/kingdom. So the care of the heart is paramount to the survival of the queen/kingdom, *us*. The subtle body heart is neither full nor empty. It is a sacred space that allows all emotions to move through it without holding onto any of them. When emotions get stuck, the start of illness, or *dis-ease* begins. You might ask, how do stuck emotions create illness? Stuck emotions contract the flow of our auric layers, slow the spin of our chakras, block the meridians, and lessen the life force in our body. The sparkle in our eyes fades, and we begin to fade away. Whatever we name that heartbreak—whatever story we attach to that event—the fact remains that our heartbreak starts to restrict the flow of vitality through us. Our body adapts and we repattern our behavior accordingly; sometimes we don't even notice the change.

When we paint from the heart, we allow our feelings, emotions, and stories to just flow. We simply allow the joy of creative movement to start rebalancing and to enliven us again. We allow the tending of our heart to keep us fully alive.

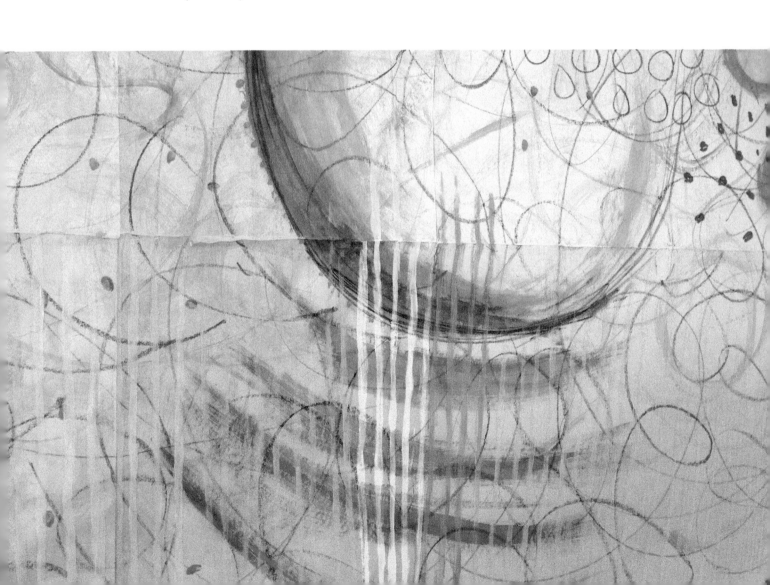

Mind: The critic

The critic? What does it mean to face the critic? We all have an inner critic. It's what keeps us within *safe* limits of societal norms. That is all fine until we have a growth spurt. Then our critic tries to limit us, to keep us in a box, and to prevent our personal growth.

We admonish ourselves by saying "I can't do that because ..."

Because why?

> You will be ... too loud ...
>
> Too big ...
>
> Too full of yourself ...

What would it be like to be really *full of yourself*?

Our deepest fear is not that we are inadequate. Our deepest fear is that we are powerful beyond measure. It is our light, not our darkness that most frightens us. We ask ourselves, who am I to be brilliant, gorgeous, talented, fabulous? Actually, who are you not to be? You are a child of God. Your playing small does not serve the world. There is nothing enlightened about shrinking so that other people won't feel insecure around you. We are all meant to shine, as children do. We were born to make manifest the glory of God that is within us. It's not just in some of us; it's in everyone. And as we let our own light shine, we unconsciously give other people permission to do the same.

As we are liberated from our own fear, our presence automatically liberates others.

— Marianne Williamson, *A Return to Love*

The critic keeps us from manifesting the glory of our light in the world. How do we recognize the critic? Knowing when the critic is present can be difficult. It's especially hard when we confront a deep-seated limiting belief. The critic can be elusive! Consider this scenario: You are happily going along, painting, writing, and feeling full of yourself. Then it starts ... hmmm ... maybe it's time for a cup of tea, a snack, wondering what is happening to the weather right now. Then you walk away...and the critic wins.

You walk away and take the pressure off of what might be a personal moment of growth; the critic survives and stops your shell from cracking open a bit more.

Sometimes the critic shows up as:

> *Oh, I should just stay were I am. Life is okay. Why try to change it? My job isn't so bad. That's why they call it work! And it pays the bills. Why dream a big dream, it just might not pan out — I will retire in say, twenty-five years. I can do what I love then! I'll keep myself small and under the radar until then.*

And so our bodies respond. Do you feel your energy deflated? Do you feel your breath slowing down? Your blood stilling and your pulse weakening? The light in your eyes dimming?

The critic can cause you to die a slow death. You attribute it to age, or to a change in your life circumstances. Before you know it, you have learned not to notice the color of the leaves, the song of the birds, the cry in your heart.

The catalyst for change has been neatly tucked away in a dusty box on the top shelf behind a book. Critic 1 — You 0.

Then one day, a photo or painting or poem catches your attention — your breath quickens, your eyes start to shine, and your true self starts to call you out into the living again.

The critic keeps you small and safe, but that is not how and why we came into this life. We are bright, shiny spirits in human form here to enjoy the gifts of being in body. No matter how you bring forth the critic: Dancing, painting, singing, or communing with nature. We are here to grow, shine, and explore this wonderful life.

It is only with the heart that one can see rightly — what is essential is invisible to the eye.

– *The Little Prince*

The first step is to recognize and acknowledge the critic. Know that it has kept you safe, and that it is part of you and your growth evolution. When you see the critic, honor it and bow to it, then put it on the shelf and move forward.

Body: A call and response with you and yourself

We are so programmed to trust our analytical mind over anything else that sometimes we don't realize we are steamrolling over a feeling that starts in our belly. The belly brain is the first place that we register a feeling, much sooner than the brain registering a feeling.

How about "Trust your gut" or "Trust what you feel"? How many times has someone said these things to you? How often do you trust your

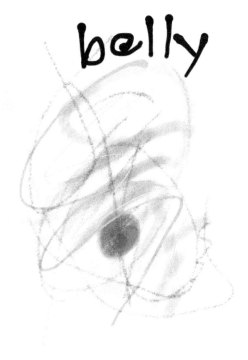

"draw me a picture of how your belly feels"

feelings or intuition? Just like building muscle strength, you need to build your intuitive trust strength. How? By practice, of course, and the best way to build your intuitive belly brain muscle is with intuitive painting. There is a lot of research suggesting that the first place we take in information is in our bellies, and then it goes up to our minds, which interpret what we feel. We know this is true, because we often say something like this: "Oh, I have a feeling about that." "This doesn't feel right." How do we recognize that feeling? By a body sensation.

When we block a feeling, we may get a bellyache and not know why. What has really happened is that we did not express ourselves, and now the feeling is stuck somewhere between the belly and the brain pathway. The belly brain is the place that gut information and responses come from. When we create from our intuition, we are listening deeply from our heart, body, feelings, and belly brain. That information gets translated into color, shape, and form. So trust the brush (or your hands, or fingers, or your body).

Don't try to figure out why—that is part of the mind's world. Remember, we have asked the mind to go on vacation for a little bit while we create. Forget about the story—just be in the flow. Follow the call and response of your inner muse.

> *Call ... "Paint red in that corner."*
> *Response ... "Okay, I'll get red. Done."*
> *Call ... "Make stripes over there."*
> *Response ... "What color? Yellow? Done."*

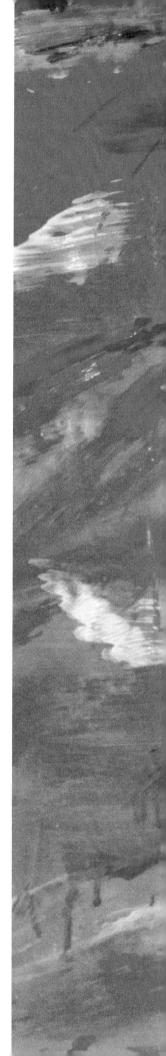

Call ... "Blue spirals everywhere."

Response ... "Everywhere?"

Call ... "Yes, everywhere"

Response ... "Woooohoooo!"

And you are happily going along; there is a lot of movement and aliveness — dare I say — fun!

Call ... "Paint a pony."

Response ... SKREEEERCCHHHHHHHH — HALT! "I can't draw a pony."

(WARNING, WARNING! Body stiffens, breathing goes shallow, belly tightens! All signs that the mind/critic is kicking in.)

Response ..."Okay, pony it is."

(Body signs are gone.)

You go on and on. Listening, uncovering, reacting, responding. Letting your creative self speak without judgment or criticism, in a call and response with yourself — belly to brush.

As you listen and trust your intuition, it will tell you what to do next, and you will get lots of aliveness/energy to do it. Intuition speaks to us in the language of color, shape, form, notes, and movement. So listen deeply, then respond, follow the energy, and keep going. Don't focus on the story, just go on the journey.

Intuitive creation is all about the **process**, not the end result.

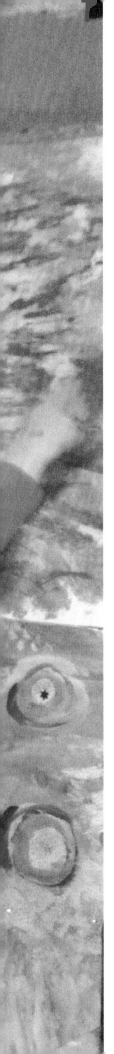

Painting Guidelines

Intuitive painting goes beyond gathering up tools and paint or learning how to master your creative hand. This chapter introduces guidelines to keep you feeling safe, grounded, and in the flow. It's time to build a safe playground for your creative muse to come out and play.

Creating your own creative womb

Setting up your creative space can be as simple as using your kitchen table, the back of your bedroom door, or a room that you can call your own. You want a private place where you can be alone with yourself — free of distractions, radio, TV, and any interruptions. *Your creative womb.*

This is your time, and your space to drop down, relax, and listen deeply. Set up your sacred space in any way that is meaningful to you. Make a special area to place objects, pictures, or words that inspire you. Bring in some flowers or greenery. As always, let your intuition be your guide.

Set up an environment for the Divine to **whisper** the truth of who you are and create it.

Change the space from day-to-day ordinary to extraordinary. Here are some suggestions to stimulate all your senses:

- Light a candle (see).

- Smudge the room with white sage, orange spray, or any other scent that uplifts the room (smell).

- Sing a song or ring a bell (hear).

- Welcome your creative self, your muse, your inner four-year-old, your playful, fearless, curious self.

- Give a great hug of appreciation to yourself for showing up and giving yourself some you time, some precious self-discovery time.

Honor all that shows up. May your intuitive creative heart lead you to new discoveries of your magnificent self.

Where to paint

Painting upright allows your body to move more. It keeps you from getting myopic and *looking at or inspecting* your paintings too much, which will instantly bring your *mind* into play. You can tape your paper to the back of a door, or you can get a large sheet(s) of double-ply cardboard and secure it on the wall to paint larger. You can use a large drawing pad or book and angle it so that you can comfortably stand and paint on your table or counter.

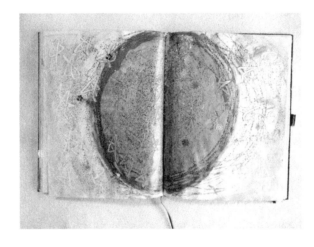

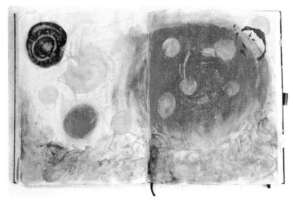

Put your roots down

It is essential to be grounded fully in your body, which allows you to be mindful and focused in your life and take clear actions. Scattered thinking or daydreaming pulls you away from the present moment. The more grounded you are, the more present you are with your feelings and actions.

I lose track of time, more often than I choose to admit to myself. I daydream, problem solve, follow my monkey mind. That's a problem. I realize that my mind gets caught up in creating a story of what comes, next instead of listening to my body, my heart.

To fully be present to myself, I need to stay grounded. Especially during the intuitive creative call and response. The more opening I leave for my creative self to come forth, the more I need to be grounded and present in what my body has to say.

ENERGY EXERCISE

Grounding

Sit or stand with your feet flat on the ground (shoes off, if possible). Imagine roots coming from the bottom of your feet deep into Mama Earth. Imagine your roots wrapping around the inner core of Earth. Feel your toes gently mimicking that wrapping sensation. Notice the tug as your body aligns and grounds into the Earth's core energy.

Feel your intake of breath moving though your lungs as it travels down into your belly. Bring your breath all the way down into your feet. Let your new, invisible roots extend out and down deeper with each breath into the core of the Earth, solidly rooting you.

As you breathe out, allow the energy from the Earth to come up your new roots, to your feet, and then into your belly. Do this for nine cycles. Feel yourself grounding and coming into the present moment.

Better?

Guidelines for creative freedom

As you paint from your intuitive feeling place, let your unconscious be your guide. Things may not look like they are supposed to (according to your inner critic), or they may look like something a two-year-old did. Even better.

Expression is what we are looking for, not perfection.

This is a process-oriented creative experience. The only thing that is important is that you have fun, listen deeply, and bear witness to yourself, one brushstroke at a time.

A judgment-free zone: One of the most important guidelines is to create a space that is safe — safe for you to explore your inner creative voice. A place where you can paint anything you want to paint without comment or judgement.

Silence or music? Music is powerful and will evoke a range of emotions. Painting in silence will allow you to deeply listen to your inner muse, without influence from outside stimulation. If you decide that you want to create with music, be mindful of your choice.

A chatter free zone: Small talk will distract you from what you are feeling. If you are painting with a friend, save the small talk for before or after your creative time.

Don't cover anything up: Everything that shows up during the creative process and on your painting is part of you, warts and all. Something may show up when you paint that you don't like. Or a drop of paint fell in the wrong place, just let it be. This is a time to explore,

be messy, and follow the energy of your emotions. A drop of paint is a drop of paint. The learnings about yourself come when you look at your reaction to that drop of paint or what you want to cover up. To cover up or make something look better is the critic's influence. *Process, not product, is the goal.*

We are an outcome driven society. From a young age, we have been urged to make a project in school and then take it home to show our parents, get it hung up on the fridge or some other place of honor. Did we create to get a gold star? Did we dance or play an instrument just to show our family or guests?

Let's reverse gears and focus on just the process. How do you feel about creating something just for you? For you and for your eyes only. Scary? Powerful? Confusing? Freeing? Liberating?

As you explore your inner landscape, your focus is inward.

Ruin it early... ruin it often

I borrowed this great phrase from my colleague, Chris Zydel. Chris is an experienced and renowned process painting facilitator. In classes, she always encourages students to ruin it early and ruin it often. I painted for many years with Chris facilitating the class, and every time I painted I understood this simple phrase more deeply.

Going deeper often means changing or ruining what has already been created. Ruin it early and often is a constant reminder of nonattachment.

Remember:

Perfection is not important.

Liking the way something looks is not the goal.

Making something look like it **should** look is not
the priority.

An example of nonattachment at its best is watching the sunset. We
are completely in the moment and accept that the light, color, temperature, and our own feelings about the day ending are all changing
and shifting from one breath to the next — then it's gone.

Honoring, listening, and responding to your inner creative self and
what your body, mind, and spirit are feeling, then expressing those
feelings via your creative self is the priority.

I am not suggesting that you should rip up your painting as a way to
ruin your painting. Rather, try to explore with paint on paper the emotions that make you want to rip up your painting. Is the critic kicking
in? Ask your intuitive self how the energy of wanting to tear up your
painting would appear as color, shape, or form. Listen to your first
impression of what to do next. Follow where the energy leads you. It
doesn't need to make sense, and you certainly don't need to know the
next step after that. Stay in the present moment, and stay with the
first hunch you get. Call and response. Call and response.

Rip, tear, and scream

I witnessed a painter truly having a battle with herself and with her painting. She was throwing paint, hitting the paper, and screaming and yelling at her painting. After a few minutes of letting her express herself, I went over and asked her to tell me about her painting. She said that she hated it and wanted to tear it up. Why tear it up? *It's ugly. It makes me mad.* Ugly (that's the mind). What are you feeling inside you? *Ugly, stupid, and really mad.* Okay, instead of tearing the painting up and screaming at it, can you move those emotions with paint via color, shape, and form? *All I want to do is tear it up.* I understand how you feel. If you tear it up, the critic wins. It would serve you better to paint this through and move all this energy stuck inside you. *It's a black brown mess.* Yes, and it is filled with all this anger. How can you make it uglier? *What!* How can you go toward the anger, the mess? The ugly? *Yellow. I can add yellow to it.* Great. At this moment, all you have to do is put yellow on your pallet. And wait for the next color, shape, and form to move you on.

Remember: don't get caught up in the story. The most important focus is to stay in touch with your present feelings, body sensations, and what your intuitive self calls for in the next step.

Here is another good example of a painting process story.

I taped up three long pieces of paper and started painting away — splattering and drawing into the wet paint with the pointy end of the brush. I gave myself golden locks and big eyes. Then mist came in, as a glittery-white-silver color that moved over the top three quarters of the painting. No judgment. Just following my creative call. I heard "paint red on — purple on — glitter glue — scrape the paint". Then the paper tore accidentally in two different places while I scraped into the paint! I consoled myself by saying, "Don't be attached. Don't freak out. The paper just tore." I told myself to keep following the energy of the brush, stay curious and interested. I found myself adding black and brown handprints crawling all over the painting — up, up, up into the mists. Then my inner critic shouted, WOOOOO STOP! (Here was my growing place). I loved the white mist and silver spatters. I loved the story that I was creating. "I can't put a big old black messy handprint up there!" My critic kicked in and told me how beautiful the white mist was. I didn't want to *ruin* it. "It will be okay if I stop here," said the critic. And I did.

I got caught up in the story. The painting was showing me my next growing place — that place of *resistance* that I called "ruining it" was stopping me from learning a lot about myself.

The intuitive creative process is like a meditative practice. Breathe in, breathe out, don't follow the mind. The truth is that every time you add a brushstroke you are *ruining it*. Every brushstroke takes courage. All you need to do is follow the brush, let your intuitive self hold the broader, bigger perspective of your healing and your journey to self discovery.

Critic changing roles: Sometimes I call the critic the saboteur. The critic always makes sure everything is just so. The saboteur will take you down to your knees when you are least expecting it. You have good intentions of refraining from junk food, for example, and before you know it, you ate a whole bag of chips, sabotaging yourself. Then the critic kicks in and says, "Told you so."

Which side is up and do you care? A different viewpoint

Sometimes shifting how you view your painting can shake up a *fixed* story, belief, or observation. You know that following your internal call and response is truly the most powerful way to explore your inner landscape.

Sometimes you get stuck in a rut, especially when you are painting alone at home. Sometimes, your mind kicks in and tells you a story. Sometimes, it tells you that this is so lovely that you can't go any further without ruining it. Sometimes, you need a new viewpoint. Try rotating your painting ninety degrees or completely upside down and begin your call and response conversation from a new angle.

Why not? It's only paint on paper. And sometimes you really need to turn your life upside down in order to see clearly.

Process, not product.

I paint in my living space. If I sit at my kitchen table, I can see my painting. Sometimes I face it, taking it in. Sometimes I have my back to it—either avoiding it, or letting my unconscious work it out. Often, there is an incubation period: I am still in dialogue with my painting whether I am actively painting. Waiting, for the next step, asking my intuitive creative self *what's next.*

My unconscious *knows*. My heart knows. My mind just has theories.

Body sensations and the creative act

We all recognize how we feel in our bodies when we feel good, happy, in the flow. We are fluid, curious, exploring, smiling, and twinkling. In short, we are ALIVE. These feelings can be present when we take a walk, read a good book, learn something new, have a great conversation, create with someone, or perform an act of kindness.

The body **doesn't** lie, only the mind.

ENERGY EXERCISE
Looking to your body

Close your eyes for a moment. Remember one of your alive moments. Let your *bodymindspirit* and your cellular memory recall how you felt then. Scan your body and allow that alive feeling to fill you up. Now shift your thoughts to a memory of being talked down to, in a subtly condescending way. So subtly that it took you a few minutes to realize something didn't feel right. Go ahead, feel that now. Your body has that memory stored. Now scan your body. Where does your awareness go? It might be very subtle, like a slight headache, or lower back tightness, or your left big toe presses against the floor. Now bring your awareness deeper into that body area. What is the color that arises from that body part? Put that color on your palette and begin to paint with it. Trust your deep inner self to guide you and your brush. Your *bodymindspirit* self will work out those feelings and sensations with your unconscious intuitive self. Invite your mind to stay out of the way.

Remember, even if that color makes no sense to the rest of your painting, follow your intuition, not what your mind tells you. Your intuitive self is holding a bigger picture, a bigger vision for you. Feeling alive can also show up as anger, sadness, crying, fear, or wanting to run. All of these feelings have energy, juice, and aliveness.

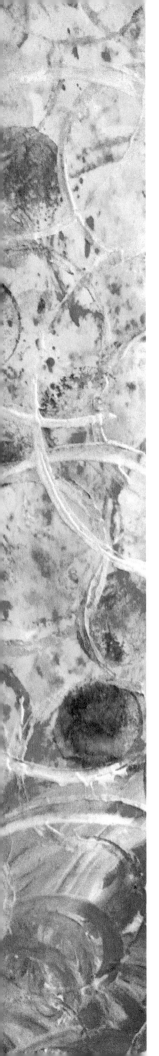

Don't judge the juice:
Follow the energy

Here the term energy is used as an action, motivator, something that excites you, that propels you, from one brushstroke to the next. Did you ever start doing something, and before you know it, hours have passed? That is because you had *lots of energy* doing the activity, so time steps off to the side for a while.

Following the energy is the real juice or motivator for the intuitive creative process. When you feel excitement or energy, follow it until it runs out, even if you haven't completed what you started. Your mind might kick in and tell you to *keep going*, you can't leave something incomplete. If there is no energy left, simply *stop* painting.

Think about it ... you are happily painting a blue circle, and all you want to do is fill your painting with more of them. There is lots of energy to keep going. You have a momentary thought (your mind) that there are too many blue circles. Check in with your intuitive self. Are you having fun? *Yes!* Then keep on moving. You may try to create a story about the circle, but there is no need to. For now, the energy is in the circle. Keep going! Let your intuition continue to download your heart's intelligence.

When the energy has left that particular movement, follow the next energy tendril. Imagine that you hear, see, feel, or sense that you need to put a pink cloud at the bottom left of your painting. Your mind may pipe up and say,

> *That defies all logic.*

Tell your mind,

Yep, I am breaking some logic right now.

Follow the energy—the why becomes insignificant.

Signs of energy: Excitement, movement, sparkling eyes, sheer pleasure of doing whatever you are doing without any good reason. Or actively avoiding a color or an area of your painting. One hour passes and it feels like only five minutes. Staying in the present moment (putting paint to paper).

Signs of NO energy: You have convinced yourself to keep going, and now you are bored. The seconds pass slowly. Your mind is wandering, you are getting tired, hungry, and disagreeable. No longer are you in the present moment. Your mind is bouncing back and forth from past to future.

To follow the energy, you must trust your creative intuitive self. As you keep following the lead from your intuition, you'll find that following gets easier. All you have to do for this moment is to paint the blue circle. Then next moment, "Paint a dog over there." It doesn't have to look like a real dog. It can be a splat of brown or a stick figure—what it looks like doesn't matter. What's important is that you follow the energy and keep moving forward.

Your intuitive self has a bigger plan in store. Your intuition's number one priority is you, your happiness, and healing the many lost or unknown aspects of yourself. How? Accept all of you, not just the parts that you want everyone else to see. Go ahead—keep following the energy.

Waylaid by the critic

How do you know when the mind or the critic has kicked in? Like any energetic cue, they range from big obvious signals to more subtle signs. Maybe the first time you get sidetracked by the critic, it's obvious. You override an intuitive *order* and you step away from your painting and say, oh, that doesn't look right, got to fix that.

Critic 1 — You 0.

Then you choose a color, for example, that fits what you are painting — like green for what you perceive is grass because grass *should* be green … right? Then you find yourself getting tired and bored.

Critic 2 — You 0.

Because you started at a young age coloring in a coloring book and when you went out of the lines, you went back and fixed them. Then your neck started to hurt.

Critic 3 — You 0.

You get the point.

The critic wants to keep you safe, by keeping you captured in a little box that I'll call your personally created limitations.

The deeper you go or the more you push against your limitations, the more the critic tries to waylay you with more and more distractions.

Sometimes you don't know that the critic won a point until you are suddenly hungry, exhausted, or you have an unbelievable urge to clean your bathroom. Anything that brings you outside yourself.

Sometimes the critic shows up as resistance. Where the simplest act of putting a colored mark on the paper feels like it will end your life (as you know it). Remember that it really is just kid's paint on paper.

Distraction = Resistance

I think about resistance as the initial signal that there is creative healing to do. If you meet resistance in your daily life, do you walk away? Push at it? Change course? Yell or throw things?

Resistance is a sign that the critic has kicked in and is trying to put you back in your self-limiting box. The critic has been charged with keeping you safe, so when you work with your unconscious self and bump into something that makes you want to run out of the room or tear up the paper, your critic comes to the rescue.

We can focus on going *toward* the resistance — painting black, adding a shape we don't like — because it's easier, at first, to face our resistance with color, shape, and form. For example, I noticed a student who had stopped painting. She had stepped back to scrutinize her painting. I asked her, "What are three things you can do to the painting?"

1. "I can add a pink flower here."
2. "I can put dots here."
3. "I can add black here. Oh, no! I don't want to paint black!"

Black it is! The place of most resistance. Because it is only paint on paper, the student filled her pallet with black and started painting. She painted through her fear and resistance to *black*.

This is a great example of how the intuitive painting experience can show you where your energy gets blocked. You can try something out with paint on paper because it is *just* paint on paper. That moment of

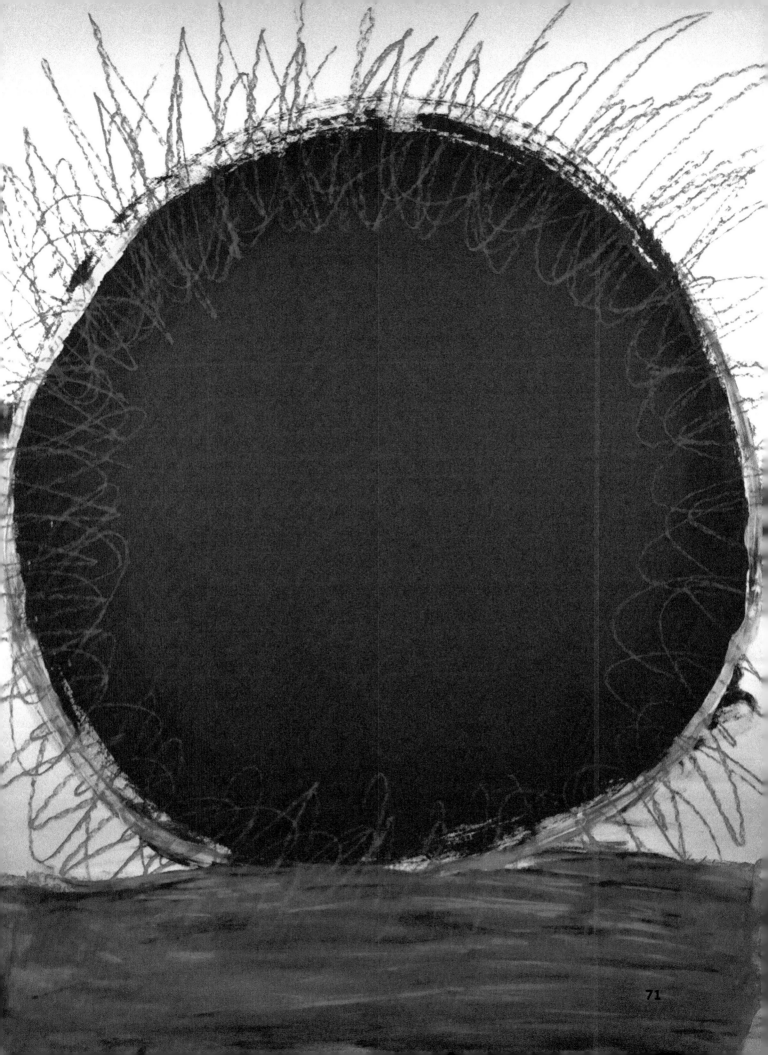

courage, pushing through a limitation, will filter through your subtle energy fields, changing and realigning your muscle memory reactions. When you meet that limiting belief in the future, it doesn't elicit the same reaction. For example, the next heart hurt that happens — you no longer hide, cover up, or get small. You no longer need to hide the raw, beautiful person that you are.

The creative healing process is one way to learn to trust your intuition and heart knowledge without judgment — to honor those raw, fragile, strong, fearless parts of you. With one brushstroke at a time, you can untangle the web of delusion you have hidden behind to keep yourself safe. Create and rewrite your story of who you are.

A little bit of understanding and healing can go a long way. This is why using your intuitive creative life force can bring forth a new you. This glimmer of understanding **unites** your physical being to your soul's truth.

The begining of a creative healing journey always looks the same: You flow with the impulse of your creative expression, one brushstroke at time. You settle deeply inside yourself and start listening to the call and response with your intuitive self. You spiral down to the center of your heart, flooding the nooks and crannies with light, curiosity, and the willingness to explore. Little by little, your unconscious shines a little light on an ouchie (limiting belief). You recognize it as X and then keep going. Sometimes you bump into big learnings and sometimes you're flooded with sheer joy and vitality because you released a stuck part of yourself.

Timing is everything

To truly honor yourself and your self-growth, you need to allow time to explore your heart. Not to be under pressure with all the other things that need to be done — such as cooking, laundry, walking the dog, sleeping, working, etc. Having this book in your hand signals that you are looking for change, perhaps craving it. Craving deep restorative you time.

A good practice is to block out at least two hours to set up your space and paint. This will give you enough time to get into a rhythm of listening deeply to your intuitive self and the rhythm of the painting itself. Each painting has its own rhythm. Some move quickly, others slowly, others are heavy, others twinkly, some are all of the above and more.

If you find yourself wanting to stop within fifteen minutes, beware. Has your critic/saboteur kicked in?

If you want to work on a painting for longer periods of time, then be sure you take regular breaks after a few hours. Without breaks, you'll get too fatigued. Your mind will kick in, and you'll hear, "Do this — no, do that ... blah blah blah." You know what happens then. The saboteur finds a way in.

How long do most people work on a painting? It varies. I have seen folks work on one painting for about an hour, or for seven days, or even everyday for months.

Students have often told me that after a series of intuitive painting classes, they felt the urge to paint daily. Their creative muscle

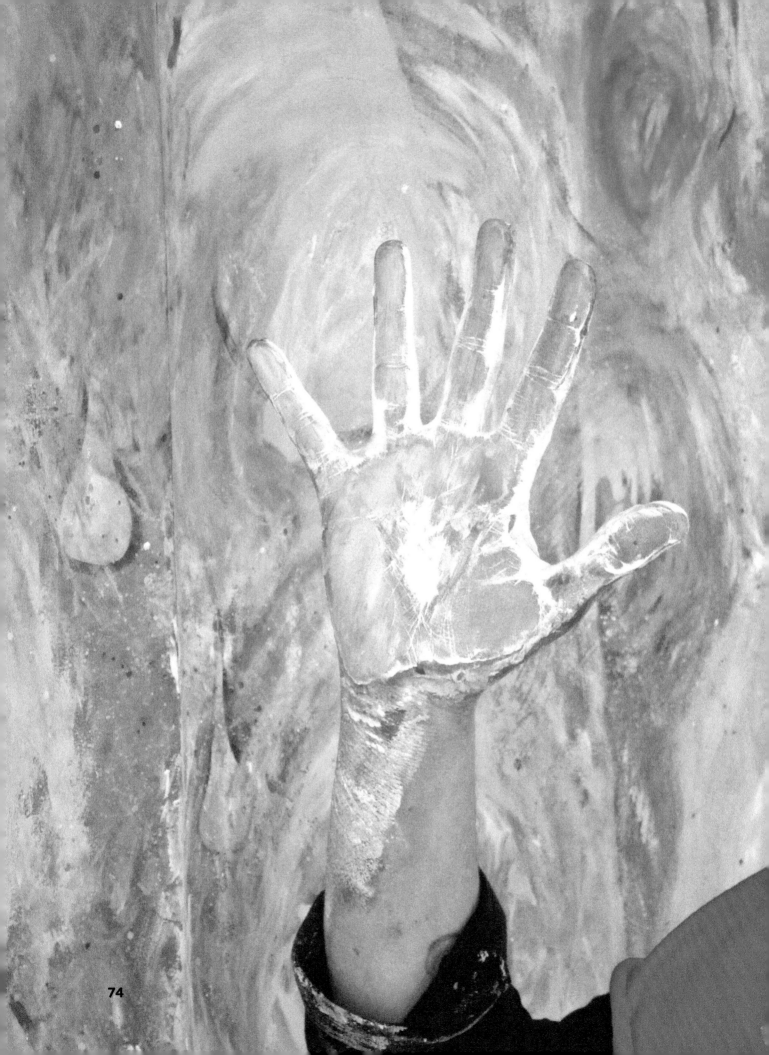

memory kicked in. Painting can be addictive — you may want to set up a regular time to paint, as we are creatures of habit. Just like taking a deep breath in — you want more.

Why not make it a good habit? Good things can happen when you do.

- Paint your heart out.

- Paint to your soul's desire.

- Paint until your eyes twinkle.

- Paint until your face hurts from smiling too much.

Am I done yet?

A painting is complete when there is no energy to do one more mark. You have called to your muse and there are no more responses. There is a sensation of stillness and completeness that moves through your body: Bliss.

Be careful that you haven't stopped early because you like the way your painting looks. You are always in control of your painting, and if you decide to stop working because you like it, then stop painting. If your heart wants to go deeper into knowing and learning about yourself, *ruin it early and often*, keep painting until there is no more energy, and you feel a sense of completion. Finally, ask yourself what are three more things you can do to the painting. You don't have to do any of them, but the question stirs the energy and you can see if there are any more marks that want to come through.

When you feel totally complete with your painting, sign it any way that you want. Sign it to own it as a part of you.

Passionate, playful, private: Sharing your paintings

Intuitive paintings are visual journals. Here are guidelines to allow others to view your paintings in a way that is safe for you:

• Share your paintings *only* if you want to and if you feel safe sharing a personal creation.

• Request that your viewer make no comments.

Even the most well-intended comment could be interpreted in a different way than the speaker intended. Even if the painter (you) wants to share the experience of creating the painting, you may want to tell your viewer, "This is a journal-like painting, and I would appreciate it if you would not make any comments about my creations." Plus, saying this is a great lesson on personal boundaries.

A student told me that she showed a painting to her partner, who had assumed that she was going to a "learn to paint flowers class." Her partner flippantly said, "Don't quit your day job!" Her partner meant it as a joke, but we are never sure how our lovely, raw, fragile self receives that message, especially if your creative intuitive self has uncovered some new understanding of yourself.

Paintings journal: There is a benefit to hanging up your paintings for a while in your home. Hanging up a painting allows you to see and learn things that you didn't see while you were painting. Viewing a

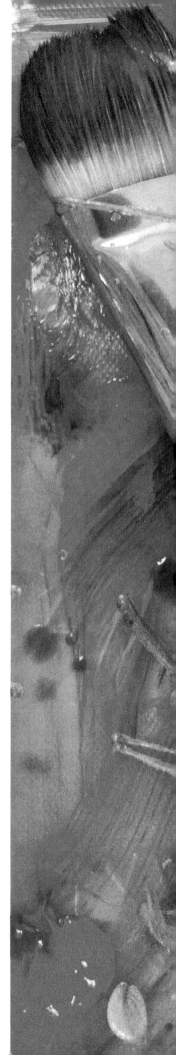

painting over time helps your *bodymindspirit* absorb more of the underlying healing that it brought up and allows more time for personal revelations to arise. The way that I like to process a painting a bit more is to write down my lessons and experiences for each painting. In fact, I have notebooks that I keep just for my painting explorations. I like to do free association writing about the painting as well to see what else my all-wise intuitive self wants to share.

As our intuitive creative healing self brings things up in manageable layers, sometimes the same theme repeats over and over again—healing little bits at a time. The learning, lessons, and healing don't end when you are done with a painting. They can live on and manifest in your day-to-day waking life, too. A journal is a great way to keep track of it all.

Love, hate, and resistance: Guidelines for when you get stuck

First, let's remember the signs of getting waylaid by the critic: feeling overwhelmed, disagreeable, bored, tired, hungry; feeling body aches; watching the clock; checking your social media; stepping back and looking and *thinking* what to do next; covering something up because you don't like it. Chances are you have bumped into something deep, and the critic/saboteur has stepped in.

CREATE

LET THE WORDS FLOW

Set up your painting space. Ground yourself.

- Grab your journal and a writing tool.

- Light a candle and make your self comfortable.

- Take a deep breath in and feel the place where your body meets the earth.

- Look at your painting and allow you eyes to soften as you take in the image.

- Ask the image what else it can share with you, and start writing.

Automatic writing accesses your intuitive wise inner self (just like when you paint). Follow the energy. Don't worry if you don't understand what you are writing; let the words flow onto the page just like paint onto paper. You don't need to make whole sentences or get the spelling right—let thoughts, imprints, and expressions flow onto the paper. If you can, don't read or edit it until the energy for writing is completely gone (just like when you paint).

If you need to add more paper, simply tape the seams together with masking tape, on the back

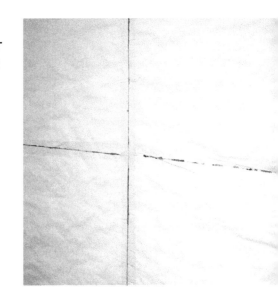

We know the critic is very tricky. Often distractions are obvious, but sometimes they are almost unnoticeable. When I facilitate intuitive painting classes, I watch closely for the slowing of energy to make sure that no one gets hung up with the critic/mind for too long.

Remember that every experience is an essential tool for learning. Learning how to come back to your truth from the critic is very important. Otherwise you may really believe what your mind tells you on your *bad* days.

Even as I am writing this section, I've gotten up three different times to do or search for something. This is my mind distracting me from talking about ways to circumvent the critic/mind.

First impression: When you realize you're getting stuck — take a deep breath, gaze at your painting with a soft nonjudgmental gaze, and feel where your attention draws you. Ask yourself, *now what?* Go with the first impression that comes to you.

Beware of conversations lead by the mind, like, *oh, if I put blue there it will balance the flow of the painting.* Or, *that doesn't make sense,* and so you change it to fit the story. Sometimes your painting is a series of seemingly disjointed images. Great! Stay with the call and response; let your creative muse keep bringing forth image, shape, and color.

Ask questions to redirect and refocus: With a soft gaze, look at your painting. Let the vibration of your painting fill your being as you look at it.

Ask yourself what three things you can do to your painting, knowing that you don't have to do any of them. Name them or write them down. Which of the three suggestions excites you, brings a twinkle to your eyes, raises your eyebrows? Which one makes you recoil, walk away, or shutdown?

Sometimes you will go toward the excitement, and sometimes you go toward what you resist the most! After all, it's only paint on paper.

CREATE

THE BODY KNOWS

Invite your body and your painting to mirror each other.

- Gaze at your painting with soft eyes, then close your eyes and do a body scan.

- Notice everything that you feel, and especially what body area has the most sensation. What place is vying for attention; it can be heaviness, achiness, even downright pain that comes out of nowhere.

- When you locate the body part with the most sensation, ask it what three things can happen in the painting. Take the one with the most energy — the most resistance or the most excitment.

- Put that color on your pallet, walk over to your painting, make a mark, and trust what shows up.

- Let your body and painting mirror and respond to each other.

The energy (excitement or resistance) is in that one color, shape, or form. That's all you have to know. Keep moving until the energy shifts to the next thing.

Creativity has aliveness to it — you can feel it in your body. When that aliveness suddenly stops, it's because you bumped into unconscious resistance. Listen to your body. It will tell you what's next as you paint and in *life*.

Let Your Creative Soul Fly!

We are the stars which sing,
We sing with our light;
We are the birds of fire,
We fly over the sky.
Our light is a voice.
We make a road for the spirit to pass over.

— Algonquin Song of the Stars

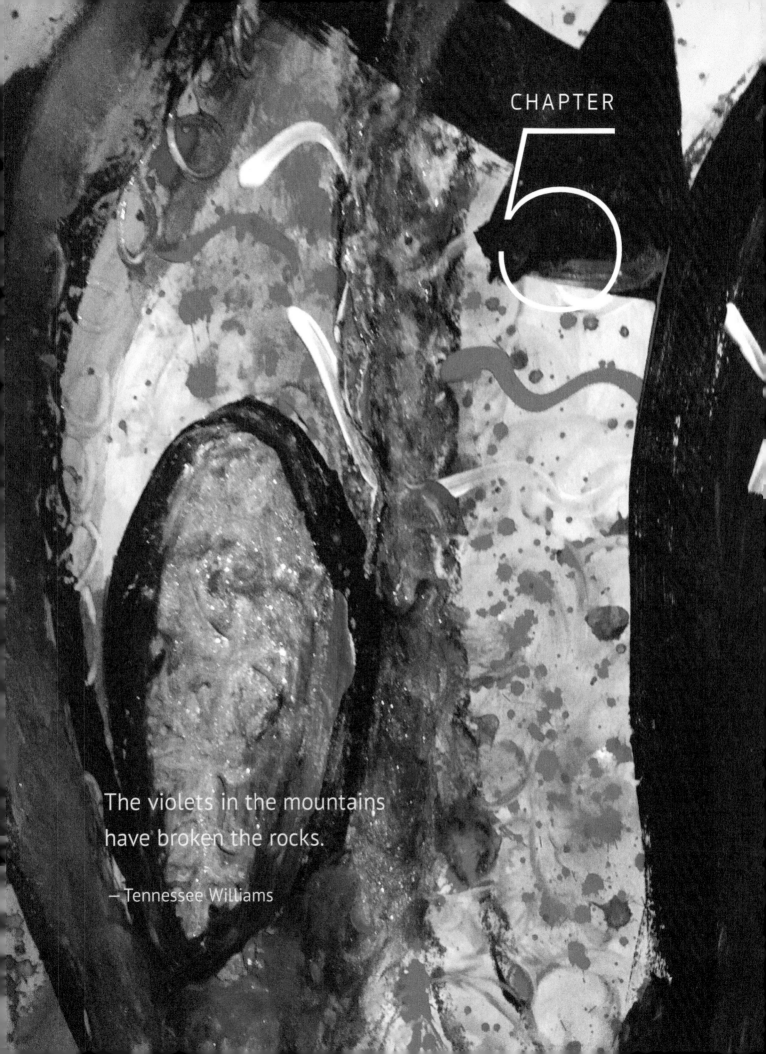

The violets in the mountains
have broken the rocks.

— Tennessee Williams

Wake Up

This section has a series of warm-up exercises to let your creative spontaneous soul take flight. Since you are not learning a fine art painting technique, you will need some new ways to learn how to listen, feel, and sense what your intuitive self has to say while painting.

It is easy, while exploring the exercises in this book, to fall back into old familiar ways of doing things. Until your *bodymindspirit's* neural pathways get rewired, your body will go back on automatic pilot. These warm-ups will rewire your go-to ways of being in the world; creating and opening up new possibilities to do something very differently than you have in the past.

Body talk

What is our body? A vessel that carts our *soulspirit* around? A series of neurological commands that moves our bones, flesh, and tendons?

Not only does our body move us around, it also allows us to feel and emote in complete union with our mind and spirit. Holistic medicine looks at our whole system as one complete unit, our *bodymindspirit*. We can have body pain because of an emotional issue or a structural reason. I liken physical symptoms to warning bells for underlying issues. For example, headaches or prolonged sadness can make you fatigued. There are myriad reasons that our bodies show us warning lights of imbalance, such as eating too many sweets to address sadness, shame, or stress. Your *bodymindspirit* will also show you warning signs when you deny an important feeling — let's say your love to create. (Of course, I would bring this up, since this is a book about creativity!) When you deny yourself an activity that you love to do, your *bodymindspirit* will start to shut down little parts of yourself in minuscule, unnoticeable bits, until you are existing on only ten percent capacity.

When we act the way we think we should act, instead of how we feel, we stop the free flow of energy, vitality, and expression in our *bodymindspirit*. We start to slow down, using only part of our vitality, which will show up as body pain and/or emotional distress, for instance, body aches or sleeplessness. We can take a pill to make the pain go away, but healing will occur when we get to the cause, question our *bodymindspirit*, and discover where and why our energy shuts down.

One of the most powerful ways to bring your body back from the brink of a slow death is to move. Moving brings breath deeper into your body, moves blood through your muscles and ligaments (including your brain), and brings your Qi, Chi, Prana, Life force up to the surface again.

In short, to *wake up*.

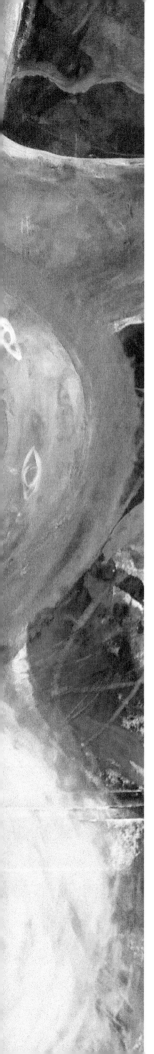

Body jazz

When was the last time you asked your elbow what it needed to say to you? When was the last time you really brought your awareness to the movement of your toes? Learning to engage your body will help you create body/feeling dialogue before pain tries to get your attention. The best way to engage your body is with movement.

My all-time favorite body warm-up music is by Gabrielle Roth and the Mirrors. The album *Initiation*, track 6 "Body Jazz." There's lots of other great music out there to dance to, but this one brings your focus to different parts of your body. If your intuition directs you to other music to move your body, as always, trust your intuition.

As you move and focus on a body part, see if a sound wants to arise. Let it rise. Let that body part release then expand with movement and sound. Move your body, your breath, and your voice. When was the last time you made a loud sound or howled? Let a sound of pleasure arise from your body, your breath, your voice. Let it out! When you create a sanctuary for creative expression, a judgment-free zone, anything is possible.

Mirror mirror

Two-pointed focus is when you hold your awareness in two places at the same time (in this case, your body and your painting). While gazing at your painting and *feeling* into your body, notice what body sensations arise.

Two-pointed focus is a great way to stay out of your thinking mind and in your body feeling belly brain. The belly brain, the first place to receive responses and feelings, sends them to the computer, your brain, to be named. Your brain then translates the sensations to a feeling word, such as happy or sad. Sometimes your brain will not recognize unfamiliar or vague feelings and you don't know why you feel what you feel, or you can't name what you feel, or you just don't feel a thing — this is where two-pointed focus can help.

Here's an example:

A student was painting for quite some time, and then she suddenly stopped. I asked,

> What is happening right now in your painting?
>> I don't know what to do.
> Okay, you don't know what to do. What do you feel when you gaze at your painting?
>> Nothing.

Bring your awareness to your body, is there any area of your body trying to get your attention? Sore, tight, tingly, pulsing?

> *Well, my neck is sore.*

Bring all your awareness to your neck — is there a color, shape, or form that that area is communicating with?

> *A pink polka-dotted cat.*

Hold that image where your neck is sore, and with a soft gaze, feel where that pink cat wants to go on your painting.

> *Top center.*

Top center. How does that feel?

> *My neck doesn't feel sore.*

Great. Go get some pink paint, put it on your pallet and follow the brush.

Two-pointed focus uses your body feelings, not your mind, to inform you where the next brushstroke will go. You can also use your body sensations to know if something feels right or not, and it can help to inform you where to paint, what to paint, and what color to choose. This is call and response from your intuitive self (in your body) to the paper. So, if you get stuck, notice if any part of your body is *speaking out*, then ask that part what it needs. Take the first suggestion even if it's ridiculous, and express it with color, shape, and form.

Avoiding the body

What happens when a concept, issue, idea, limiting belief, or expression shows up in your painting? Do you want to avoid it?

A student's first painting moved a lot of energy; big black swirls showed up as she moved with tear-filled eyes, a little rage, followed by hysterical laughter. This is not a typical experience for a new student, but clearly she was ready for a healing experience. As always, the invitation I give to folks is to *paint* and *listen* then *paint* and *listen* some more.

The very next week she was painting with a tiny brush and very large paper. Her shaky robotic-like brushstrokes revealed images of boats, pools, a canoe — lots of imagery, but not a lot of energy. When she'd painted the week before, she was engaged with her body, moving her body as she painted. This time, she held the tiny brush so tight in her grip I thought it would break. Small, disjointed images scattered across the large expanse of paper. This would not have been an issue if she hadn't been holding her body so tightly. After a while she started massaging her neck, arms, and shoulder. (Achy body parts are a sure sign that some feeling or feelings are stuck in the body.) Because this is an explorative painting process for self-discovery and personal growth, I asked her what was happening with her shoulder. She didn't even realize she was rubbing it. Her mind was cleverly keeping her unaware of her physical distress. After some conversation, I asked her to bring her awareness to her pain, walk over to the paints, pick a color, grab a brush, and express that feeling with paint, brush, and paper. Brush in hand, she allowed her body and brush to move across the paper. After some time, she finished. I asked her how her neck felt. She said, "I feel more expanded."

Yes, expanded. If you hold on too tightly, your mind will tell you a story that keeps you small, tight, and controlled, so you can't grow.

This story, my friends, is an example of a magic moment that happens when you stay open to the call and response with your intuitive self and allow whatever shows up to flow onto paper without judgment. When she left, her eyes were twinkling.

You will get exactly what you need during each creative experience, regardless if you are painting for two hours or two weeks. Sometimes the same story will show up, just with different players, or a seemingly cohesive theme will show up. Stay with what is right in front of you, don't try to steer the painting to a particular outcome.

Your intuitive self will take you just where you need to be, so you can express your heart's desire for that moment and that moment only. The whole purpose of creative intuitive painting is that you show up (just as you are) and express yourself from your authentic place. Why? The more authentic you are in life — authentically true to yourself and in the world — the better the world will be.

Shake, giggle, and move!

This book is about creativity and bringing awareness back to your body by watching and exploring your limitations. When you receive an invitation to explore your flexibility, be mindful of your current body limitations. As the musical group The Staple Singers sing, *"Respect Yourself."*

Here are a few **movement exercises** to begin a conversation with your body and a greater sense of freedom.

Body scan: Stand comfortably, with your feet hip-width apart. Keep your knees soft.

First bring your awareness to where your feet meet the earth. Feel the earth yielding to the weight of your body. Take a deep breath. Now feel the soft spot on the top of your head, open like a flower to the sun, open to the heavens, and connect to the North Star. The North Star is the center of the sky for us and is a great counterbalance to the earth's core.

When you feel grounded between earth energy and sky energy, begin to scan your body. Start with the soles of your feet, your toes, and all fifty-two bones of your feet. Then check in with your legs, lower torso, belly, back, chest, shoulders, neck, hands, arms, head. Notice what you feel: hot, cold, tingling, numb. (Don't judge, just notice.) When you feel a particularly intense sensation, ask that body part if there is a feeling attached to it. (Just notice.) The point of the body scan is to say hello to your body and ask if there is anything it needs to share with you.

Shake your jiggly parts (adapted from Carolyn Eitel): Carolyn has a great sense of humor and wit. I just had to share this with you.

In this exercise, put some music on that you love — something that you can shake to. Wiggle and jiggle all your body parts to let your entire body move and be known. Let go of body conscious society rules, and shake all your fleshier parts. Don't hold in — let loose.

Rubber spine (adapted from Linda Puerner-Fisher): Imagine your spine is fluid and feels rubbery. With slow, undulating movements, let your spine flex side-to-side, front to back. Let it be rubbery. Now take that rubbery feeling down to your legs with a gentle bounce, keeping the rest of your body soft. Bring the rubbery feeling up to your neck letting your head comfortably bobble on the top of your spine. Now bring that soft undulating feeling out to your arms and hands, letting your body stay soft and rubbery. Notice the places that you are holding tight and the places that want to release even more. Let each part release with each breath.

Yoga is a practice of mindful movement. Find a class that fits who you are. Ask your body if it wants gentle movement or more powerful movement. Let your intuition be your guide. You can do the sun salutation sequence as a nice body opening. You can find the sequence on the Internet. This is a great practice to do in the morning to wake up your body, as you greet the rising sun. Let the sun's warmth meet your body, your heart, and merge with your radiant self.

Bringing a practice of mindful yoga movement to the opening of your creative practice will open up your meridians and chakras and get all your juices moving.

Feel love and let go: Dance to Donna Summers. Yes, feel the love for your body. Feel your aliveness spreading throughout your body. Feel love and gratitude for your body, your family, your community, and the world. Dance until you can't dance anymore.

Awaken your third eye — your creative eye

Mysteries are not to be solved.

The eye goes blind when it only wants to see why.

—Rumi

The more you engage your senses, the easier it is to hear, see, feel, sense your intuitive self. Your third eye, or sixth chakra called *Ajna*, is located in the space between your eyes, where your nose meets your forehead.

The third eye is about our *inner* everything: voice, seeing, experience, intuition, sixth sense, knowing, and feeling. It is often called the psychic chakra. The French philosopher Rene Descartes believed the pineal gland, associated with the third eye, is "the seat of the soul."

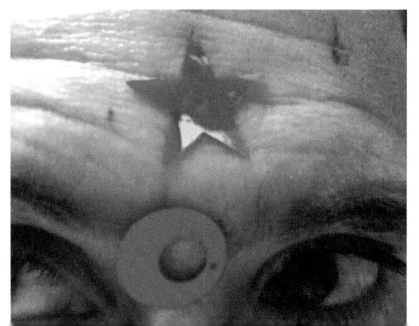

ENERGY EXERCISES

Open your third eye

Exercise ONE: Get comfortable and bring all your awareness to your breath. Follow your breath deeply into your body. Feel yourself ground into the yielding earth. Now bring your awareness to the space between your eyes, your third-eye area, and breathe into that area. With each breath feel your third-eye area starting to tingle. Start inviting your third eye to open, experience it fluttering open. This is your third-eye energy. You are always in control of how much or how little it opens. Your body knows, your mind knows, your spirit knows what is right for you. Just allow and notice.

Exercise TWO: Do the above and add very lightly tapping with your index finger on your third eye with the intention of waking it up.

Exercise THREE: There are sounds and vibrations associated with your third eye, seed sounds are vibration sounds that are said to open particular energy centers of the body. The seed sound for the third eye is Sham (Shum). Sing SHAM and direct that sound vibration up to your third-eye area. Notice what you feel and sense, what shifts in your head, your body, and your space.

Western note scale is Do (A), Re (B), Mi (C), Fa (D), So (E), La (F), Ti (G), Do (A). You can also sing or play the Western note «A» to stimulate your third eye. Again notice what shifts in you and around you as you do.

Exercise FOUR: Buzz buzz. You can also make a buzzing bee sound. Direct that sound to your third eye. The vibration will stimulate your third eye.

Other associations to help wake up your third eye:

Colors associated with this area are indigo or deep purple. You can shine a purple light on your third-eye area or wear these colors to stimulate your third-eye energy.

Gemstones associated with this area are amethyst, lapis lazuli, and sapphire. You can place one of these semiprecious stones on your third-eye area. Lie down and notice what happens to your body. You can carry one of these stones with you throughout the day or place under your pillow at night to stimulate your third-eye energy.

Flower essences associated with this area are lavender and Queen Anne's Lace. You can rub this on your skin daily or place a few drops in a bath to stimulate your third-eye energy.

Essential oils associated with this area are clary sage, lavender, and lemon. You can rub this on your skin daily, or place a few drop in the bath to stimulate your third-eye energy.

Let your intuition guide you. It's best to start simply. Let your body adjust to the energetic shifts with each experience so you can notice the shifts in your being.

CREATE

PAINT YOUR VISION

*Set up your painting space. Create your sacred space.
Ground yourself.*

Let your creative muse teach you about the energy of your third
eye by painting it.

• Do one or two of the third-eye exercises to open your
  intuitive center.

• Then stand in front of your paper and ask your third
  eye to speak to you via color, shape, and form.

• Ask your third eye to share with you what you need to
  know right now, at this moment.

• Let the vibration of color awaken your third eye.

• Let the movement of your body as you paint wake up
  the inner vision energy that lives in each cell.

• Let all of your senses invite your third eye to enliven
  you and teach you about your authentic self.

• Let your third eye speak to you with color, shape, and
  form — that powerful language of vibration that we all
  know before we learn to speak.

Make Sound!

Sound is a powerful tool to wake up the energy in your body, your mind, and your soul. Creating a sound with your voice allows your body to resonate and connect to that sound vibration and a body part, stimulating sluggish areas and breaking up stuck areas. (Think about the power of sonar—how far it can travel and how it can break up stone.)

Here are some explorations into sound that you can try—alone or in a group. After each exercise, notice how you feel—journal it, dance it, sing it, paint it.

YES... NO... I mean it!: When is the last time you said what you were really feeling? Said *yes* or *no* and really meant it? Not only is it important to have clear communication with yourself and others, but it is important to express your needs and desires to others and feel okay about it. Do you tend to be a go-with-the-flow type of person and let what you want be overridden by another? Do you say *yes* when you really don't want to? Do you say, "Its up to you," when you really mean *no*? Say *yes* with gusto and mean it! Or *no*, when you don't want to do something. Time to take your voice back and speak your truth.

In a mirror, look at yourself and say *yes* with about fifty different intentions and inflections. Say it from deep within you. From your diaphragm. From your belly button. From your pelvis. From your toes. How does that feel? How does your body feel?

Now say *no* fifty different ways. Again how do you feel? What emotions arise? Which one was easier to do? Do you feel empowered by both *yes* and *no*? Try this with a friend. Notice if you have the same commitment to the word. Does your body feel different interacting with another? Are you concerned about how the other person feels or responds?

Sing it: Sing your name. "My name is_____." Sing it loud. Sing it full. Put your soul into it! Sing how you feel "Right now I feel_____." Sing happy. Sing mad. Sing excited. Sing unsure. *Sing it loud.*

Babble talk: When I was little, my mom and I would talk to each other in a made-up foreign language. I would wander around the house babbling to the plants, the animals, and even out loud to myself. Making sounds for the sake of making them is a good way to open up your throat. Here's an example: "Fouled ooo poi u nut the roo feul foo alleow chodid naaa yaaa." Got it? Try it!

Seed sounds: There are specific sounds that will resonate, stimulate, and enliven each of your chakras. The seed sound, (rooted in ancient Sanskrit), does not have a word meaning, but matches the vibration of a particular chakra. Keep your breath smooth and bring your attention to that particular chakra. Let that sound actually vibrate in that chakra.

AUM — Crown chakra

SHAM — Third-eye chakra

HAM — Throat chakra

YAM — Heart chakra

RAM — Navel chakra

VAM — Sacral chakra

LAM — Base chakra

Healing Sounds of the Organs: In this exercise, color, sound, and movement unite. In Asian medicine, each organ has a sound and movement to keep your organs balanced and in health.

ORGAN ASSOCIATIONS TO THE HEALING SOUNDS

LUNGS	KIDNEYS	LIVER	HEART	SPLEEN	TRIPLE WARMER
Sssssssss	Woooooo	Sshhhhh	Hhaaww	Wwhhoo	Heeee
Teeth almost touching, tongue behind teeth.	Lips round, like blowing out a candle.	Lips puckered, sound rises from the liver.	Mouth relaxed, soft sigh from the heart like saying *aahh*	Lips round, throat open slightly and tense, guttural.	Lips thin, tongue almost touching the top of mouth, sound vibrating the palate.
Imagine a bright shiny white, filling your lungs.	Imagine a royal blue-black filling your kidneys (lower back).	Imagine a soft green, filling your liver (under right side of rib cage).	Imagine a bright red filling your heart (center of chest).	Imagine a bright yellow filling your spleen (under left side of rib cage).	Imagine all the colors blended together, filling your entire torso.

DrumFlower meditations (by Lesley Tao Mowat): *Tao teaches how to use sound for wholeness and healing, I love these exercises so much that I had to share them with you!*

We call this experience deep listening, shifting your primary awareness from seeing to hearing. Sound has a physical vibration we can hear and also feel. Have you ever been in a place with bass sounds coming through large speakers? You can literally feel the sound waves moving over your body. Sound is vibration … everything is vibration.

You can do sound meditations, individually or one after the other, as a flowing experience. They can be done standing or sitting. Create a space where you will not be interrupted and where you feel privacy to make these sounds without inhibitions.

Deep Listening: Ten minutes is the recommended amount of time to perform deep listening (or longer if desired).

The first thing you want to do is open up to sound. Connect your body, your mind into the spirit of deep listening. This meditation will allow you to take some time to access the sound within you and expand to the environment of sound around you.

Close your eyes, or better yet cover them with a bandana or a blindfold. You can be in any comfortable position, just take care not to be so comfortable that you fall asleep. Begin your deep listening time with a number of deep slow breaths. This will slow you down, bringing you to a more present, mindful, aware state of being. Start your deep listening right away as you take those deep breaths. Listen within yourself, inside yourself to what each breath sounds like … inhaling slowly … exhaling … listening … listening to your body. Let any outside sounds be far away and of no concern as you listen deep within. When it feels right, allow your breathing to become natural. Keep listening. When it feels right, not rushing … allowing time … shift your awareness of listening from within to the sounds coming from the environment around you. Start with your focus of awareness on the sounds close to you. Allow them to be in your consciousness, your body, your ears, by just experiencing the sounds. Don't try to name them, let the sounds wash over you. Then let your awareness move further away to the sounds in the distance. You may notice sounds you never heard before, even though you've been in this place many times. Just allow yourself to hear. Shift your awareness to focus on specific sounds. How do they make you feel? What is your experience of listening to each one? Experiment with listening in this deep way. It is a very different experience to practice deep listening in nature versus in a place with loud mechanical sounds. Find a place that can be your sound sanctuary — with loud machine sounds only in the distance, if at all.

Find your own tone and express it. Ten minutes (or longer if desired) is the recommended amount of time to express your own tone. Start by taking some nice deep breaths. Focus on each long inhalation and exhalation. After a few breaths, begin to allow a sound to happen on the out breath … a long vocal sigh at first … allow more sound to come as each out breath happens … allow it to be a natural expression of sound … it will become a tone. To find your note, experiment by starting with the lowest or highest tone you can do and then slide up or down in pitch … allowing the tone to settle in the most comfortable pitch for you at that moment. Then sing that pitch as a long tone for a full exhalation. Keep toning that same pitch until you feel complete.

Use deep listening to hear and feel that note inside and outside your body. Feel the vibration in your body. Is there a particular place you feel its focus? You may try this with different tones and notice where you feel the vibration most in your body. Which tone is *your tone* on a given day? This will change. You can also experiment with sending the vibration of that tone to parts of your body or finding tones that vibrate different areas in your body.

When you feel complete with your sound making, lie down in silence for about ten minutes. Be the watcher. What is happening in your body? In your mind?

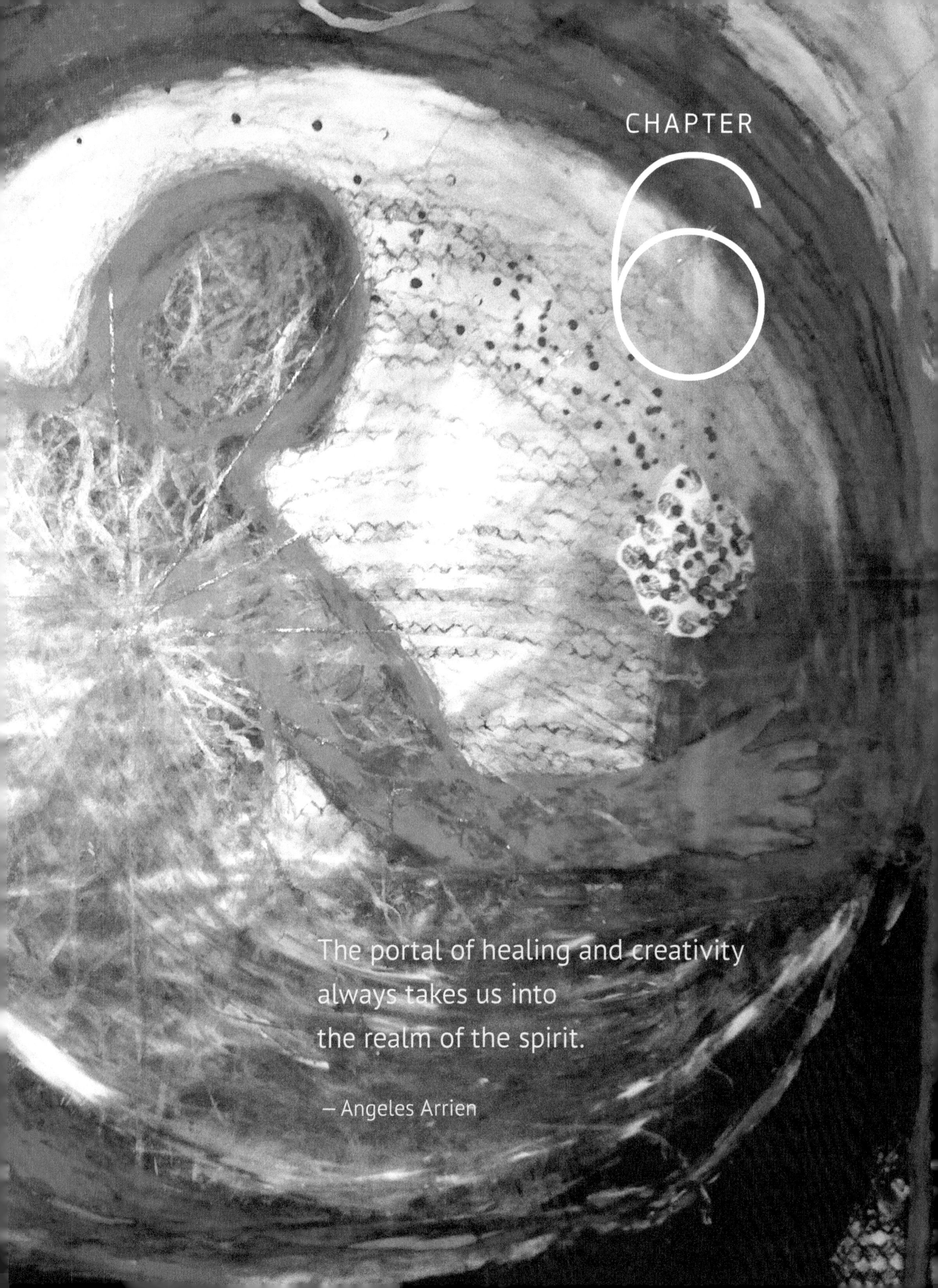

CHAPTER

6

The portal of healing and creativity
always takes us into
the realm of the spirit.

— Angeles Arrien

Coming Back to Yourself

How is a simple act of creativity a path toward healing? Healing is a constantly evolving experience, and there are many levels in which healing can happen:

In your body — gut, bones, sometimes organs, blood, nerves

In your mind — memory, the ability to think clearly, the ability to sleep well

In your spirit — feelings, a peaceful versus a wounded heart, happiness versus sadness, and joy versus grief

Creative healing takes you on a journey to transform your limiting beliefs, those stories that stop you from living fully.

Over time, hurts to your mind, heart, and body distort and unbalance the manifestation of your original energy blueprint, and can lead to chronic pain. In order to heal, you need to look deeply, be compassionate with yourself, and trust in the healing process. Thank goodness that your intuitive self knows where to start.

The intuitive healing process is slow, deep, beautiful, and **unfolding** from one moment to the next.

True healing takes time and requires **care and love** for and from yourself.

You are born with a heart that knows your life's purpose. Over time, you experience dings to your heart. Whether big or small, you register these dings as hurts. These hurts are held in cellular memory, creating a holding pattern, called pain. Sometimes, that pain is a holding pattern in a *body/organ*, which might appear as unexplained lower back pain. Sometimes the pain is in the mind and shows up as a limiting belief such as not feeling good enough. Other times the pain shows up as an *emotion* such as hopelessness. The good news is that the creative process is one of the many ways to heal this pain.

Creative healing: What does it look like?

The cycle and rhythm of energetic healing is the same whether it is with holistic healing or with the intuitive creative process. When I first saw the energetic rhythm that happens during the intuitive creative process, I recognized the same healing pattern that happens in an acupuncture session. The *bodymindspirit* receives an invitation to

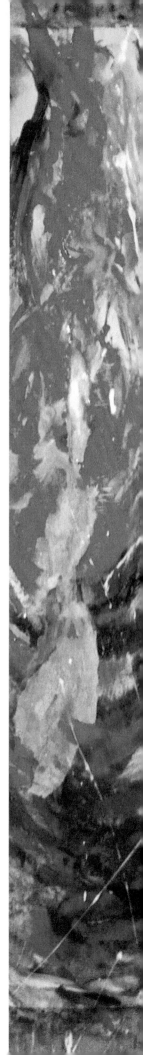

move back toward harmony. (All disease comes from being out of balance, off center, askew). First there is an invitation, then a glimmer of understanding, then rebalancing in the subtle energy body systems that informs the bones, cells, mind to change, which makes the heart unencumbered and able to shine brightly.

Here is an example of a healing session: Someone comes in for treatment of chronic back pain. They tell me that they are beside themselves with too much work. They sit in front of a computer all day, often work late into the night, and don't see this relentless pattern changing in their future. They are off center, mentally and spiritually drained; they need hope, a plan, and reassurance that their burden will change. This particular person is also a pleaser and will not say *no*. As their back gets better, they come back into center more. They are able to have a vision of change, rest, relaxation, and make choices that are right for them.

Similarly, in the intuitive healing creative process, you invite your inner four-year-old out to have fun and allow space for your creative life force to move — which brings forth pure joy, a twinkle in your eyes, and a smile in your heart. Loads of revitalizing, feel-good energy is released through the body, enlivening your *bodymindspirit*. What a profound, powerful experience! As this creative feel-good energy moves through your being, you begin to let go of the *should haves* and *could haves* that weighed you down. The process is much like removing the fine layers of an onion; stress and worry start to fall away from your subtle body energy as your inner landscapes are revealed. As you paint more, you start to dip a little deeper into your unconscious self, exploring those previously hidden hurts, uncovering, realigning, healing, and enlivening.

Fortunately, your intuitive creative soul guides the healing process. You go downward into your unconscious, and find a hidden hurt that is ready to start healing, that speaks to you in the language of color, shape, and form. If you focus on the color/shape/form in front of you, without adding a story or being attached to the outcome of your process, then a glimmer of healing will come forth.

Your intuitive self sets the pace for your healing, showing you the hurt in color, shape, and form. Notice it, feel it, acknowledge it. Then your *bodymindspirit* muscle memory starts to come into balance. The joy of your heart carries the momentum, righting your *bodymindspirit* muscle memory. That new true healing information then flows back into your bones, muscle, mind, tendons, and feelings. As your body brings forth this new healing, it simultaneously realigns how you are out to the world *(As within, so without)*.

Performing this deep exploration doesn't mean that you release old hurts all in one fell swoop — you wouldn't be able to process the overload. Your job, during this creative healing experience, is to allow your experience to unfold slowly and safely over time, by letting your unconscious self lead the way. You never want to rush in and remove the traumas forcefully, which is like constantly reopening an old wound, which causes more trauma than healing. You won't learn anything new about yourself if you are retraumatized. Your unconscious intuitive self is profoundly intelligent and allows little bits of understanding to surface while you create, always in chunks that you can understand and integrate. You will not be overwhelmed with a realization or be retraumatized. You always will receive what you can handle.

Unconscious memory: Little bits of understanding come up, and those glimpses heal your old hurts. You only need a small bit of understanding to start your healing process. That understanding can be a dot, a green line, something seemingly insignificant, which can act as a catalyst to harmonize the system back to a healthier pattern — little by little, brushstroke by brushstroke. As you shift and clear layers of those old patterns, you make room for the parts of yourself that you have put away in the shadow space to integrate into your *bodymindspirit.*

I like to envision this type of creative healing as *shining a little flashlight on a hurt* that you have put off to the side or compartmentalized. That beam of light from your flashlight, light as a form of understanding, has the power to transform anything. Unconscious hurt to conscious healing. What a purely alchemical healing moment!

The story of who, what, when, where your hurt arose is not important. Neither are the patterns of cause and effect. You can't let the story stop your flowing life. You must focus on what is important: your call and response with paint on paper. That's where your healing *arises and evolves.*

Changing a learned behavior

Once, at an intuitive painting retreat, I stopped painting because I started to feel crabby. I realized the crabbiness was a reaction in my *bodymind* to something that the painting was bringing up. The facilitator asked me what was going on. After some soul searching, I found that what I needed was more paper—*to go bigger*. My unconscious was inviting me be as big as I wanted to be. My old belief was to stay small; my inner creative self wanted me to go BIG. With paint on paper, I got to experience what is was like to take up lots of space and be big while in the safety of the creative womb. In the studio, I got to safely explore *big*. My *bodymindspirit* cellular memory held that experience. Then as I moved out into my day-to-day world, my energy began seeking out ways for me to show up big!

True healing occurs when we **come back** to ourselves, accept who we are (imperfections and flaws), share ourselves with the world, and live authentically with joy.

Moving from the inside out to the world — how painting can be healing: Since we are energetic beings in an energetic world, we must consider resonance, which is the energy inside of us being reflected outside of us, a kind of energetic mirroring. Learnings that shows up during a painting exploration will show up in your day-to-day life. This gives you the opportunity to allow your *bodymindspirit* muscle memory pattern to integrate with your everyday life.

Recurring healing themes can show up for long periods of time. You can see a change in yourself soon after your painting epiphany, or you may recognize that you are different many weeks, months, or years after your creative healing. The beauty of unconscious healing is that as you are creating, you are unaware of what belief is being healed. You don't have to *know*. You can expand and let your creative life force move more fully through you. Your unconscious will emerge with little bits of realizations and healing through color, shape, and form. All you have to do is be willing to let your creative light shine. Then open the door of your heart and let it shine.

I love the way this Painting makes me feel

Often folks walking through the studio say, "Wow these paintings are great!" or "This room feels fabulous." They are responding to the energy of *creative freedom*. Intuitive painting exudes a sense of aliveness, a vitality that emanates from paintings that hang on the wall. Yes, all art has energy, but intuitive creations always have a noticeable life force radiating from them, because they are a pure response from your creative life force and your heart.

One reason that intuitive creations shine with aliveness is that they are not censored. They are pure energetic expressions—often outrageous, big, bold, and far from perfect—created with wild abandon. It is the glimmer of your true self, shining, radiating, gushing, rushing forth, coming back into your life—with every brushstroke.

Have you ever tried to create something perfect, doing the same thing over and over again, wanting to make it just right? If so, then you remember how your attempts to create perfectly took all the fun and excitement away. It became stiff and barely alive. When you are *not* thinking about *product*, the desire to create something perfect or nice is not important. Your creation can pulse and breathe with life force and vitality.

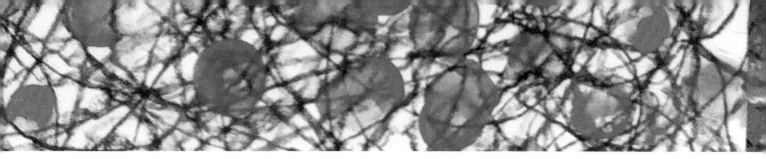

Training wheels for life

The painting process is a way to work through old societal programs and release the energy that keeps you stuck. Examples of society's programs are girls should wear pink and boys blue. Sometimes a societal pattern that no longer serves you, or actual memories get released. Change occurs when you allow yourself to be present to everything that you experience with love and compassion — accepting your fear, rage, beauty, shame, vulnerability, and grief. Be present with all the parts of yourself, express them creatively; then transformation and healing starts.

When some of your old programming gets cleared away, that space is filled with your own vibrant, vital, creatively alive true self. This creative healing process connects you directly with your creative Source, which allows you to access the joy, pleasure and *the point of greatest aliveness* that is your birthright as a human being.

In shamanic healing, rediscovering your vitality means that you retrieve or recover the lost, tucked away parts of your soul. You come back to your whole essential self and live from a more authentic you. Your creative self will invite you to try on a new way of being — like being really big. Or making noise, painting red, getting messy, or dancing naked — all with paint on paper.

You may meet something in your creative process that stops you —
for instance, maybe you just don't like the color black. You would do
anything to avoid painting black. But here's the deal: you can explore
your personal taboos safely; it's just paint on paper. If you don't
like it — you can stop. But why not go toward the things you avoid
the most? It's safe, and no one will get hurt. You are in complete
control. You can walk away. You can forge onward, move past your
resistance, and change those old muscle memories. You can move
toward harmony.

Happy accidents

When you completely let yourself follow the call and response of your
creative self, you may end up putting a green square here, and a few
moments later you have to put a tree over there. Then, some time
later, in complete abandon with your creative muse, you put a red line
on the green box. Always following the energy ... not the story.

A while later, you are looking at the green box with the red line on it,
and it makes sense. You would never have thought of painting what
showed up, but you did, and you have a lovely memory from long ago
that brings a little bit of happiness back to you. A little bit of your life
force comes flooding back to you.

Here's another example. You are painting swirls, and accidentally
cover something up in all that energy. At first you are upset because
you've covered something up that you liked, then it frees up some old
memories of feeling shamed. It doesn't matter if you painted swirls or
a daisy.

What you paint doesn't matter as much as **how you feel** when you are painting.

You saw it. You felt it in your *bodymindspirit*. That memory of shame starts to heal. That memory of shame loses its subconscious charge in your being — little by little — brushstroke by brushstroke.

You cannot control the intuitive painting process. Oh, you can try; the mind is so clever. But for deep revelations and healing, trust the brush!

Your inner muse creates a happy accident to override your mind so you can shine a little light on a memory and bring about healing. Healing results in more life force.

Giving your muse freedom

You've probably heard these expressions: Children should be seen but not heard. Be quiet, you're too loud. You're too rammy. Be ladylike. Act like a man. Big boys don't cry.

All of these expressions are constraints to keep you within the societal norm. Most of these words of social etiquette come from a place of fear. If you are noticed, you will be seen, which stems from our evolutionary history. If you are noticed, some larger animal will eat you. The limbic system of our brain gets turned on at six weeks in utero, and it doesn't fully develop a filter until we are born. Which means we absorb and carry every feeling around us until we are born. Yikes! An emotion can get stuck in our survival system so deeply that we often don't know what is true and what is not true. You can see how these deep-seated fears can get caught in our thought programs and then are passed on for generations without anyone ever realizing where they started.

How does your *thought programming* fit into this intuitive creation book? We have all received messages that were originally designed to keep us safe, but now hold us back from expressing ourselves fully. Within the safety of the creative process, you can explore all of your taboos and rules with paint on paper. You guys out there: Would you ever publicly admit that you like to paint in pink? Gals, what would happen if you say you hate flowers or babies?

The removal of taboos can radically change your life view.

When you follow your intuitive, true self in a step-by-step exploration of your personal taboos, using paint and paper — no one gets hurt, no feelings get overridden. You can think or act however you want. You get to explore what is in front of you.

Slowly, with one brushstroke at a time: you can be

> As big
>
> As wild
>
> As loud
>
> As messy
>
> As unconventional, as you want to be.

How does that make you feel? Awake, alive, curious, terrified?

In this creative process, accepting all parts of yourself is key! Your creative, judgment-free zone is a safe haven for however you feel at the moment.

You begin to accept the: happy, jiggly, fat, skinny, masculine, feminine, shy, angry, introvert, extrovert, bitter, sexy, powerful, messy you. It's just paint and paper after all.

Be radical — **accept** and love all parts of you.

Your personal mythology

We all have an individual visual language. Poets have a style or voice; the same is true for painters and musicians. When it comes from your true authentic self, your individual visual language or mythology is as unique as you are.

The intuitive creation process doesn't require any skill. You just have to know how to listen, to follow what your inner creative self calls for you to do. You might notice that particular images show up — or that there is a particular way you apply the paint, use a drum, or dance.

When you are creating, try not to get caught up in the story or analyze your images. Instead, just let them flow. Just like layers of paint, sound, or movement, layers of healing blossom with each call and response from your intuitive heart.

The first step is allowing!

Our expressive freedom arises from how we feel and listen without any concern for right or wrong. We are all so hardwired to do the *right* thing, sometimes it brings out our inner perfectionist.

Watching clients get stuck by their inner perfectionists has made me question the impact of coloring books. When we are about two- and four-years-old, we are given crayons and paper and told to *go for it*. Somewhere between four- and six-years-old, we are given coloring books and told to stay within the lines. Then we are told the sky should be blue, and the grass should be green. Slowly, very slowly, our creative freedom gets culled — tight — recognizable — obvious — normal. We start to move through life within the black lines, following the rules.

Oh, don't get me started here! Have you noticed that there are now separate toy aisles for girls and boys? The girls' toys are mostly pink and sparkly; the boys' toys are brown, blue, and black. Since when have we allowed commerce to have so much power over who we are? (Yes, this started in the 1950s, but it feels over the top now.) Sorry for the soapbox, but this programming is another prison sentences, of *should be's*, and taboos — just like staying small, and good.

Intuitive creative work is a step-by-step, breath-by-breath experience — exploring those boundaries and feeling what it's like to step over those lines, one breath at a time. One color, one beat, one step, one word at a time.

You may have a personal mythology, but you don't need to maintain a style as professional artists do. You know a Bach or Angelou or Warhol, by their consistent style. Was this their original voice? Perhaps, but I wonder if they didn't sometimes just stop there because that is what everyone else thought was unique and original. The difference between our creative process here and the commercial artistic world is that we don't stop exploring our individual mark; we don't get stagnant. The way we create here is by being constantly alive, remaining open to whatever shows up, and bringing more and more of our life force to the surface so we can truly be ourselves, free of *the shoulds*.

As you create and your personal mythology emerges, allow it to change and morph as you explore. Don't lock yourself into any box. Allow for growth in your process. Allow for change to arise from deep within you.

GROWTH=CHANGE=HEALING

Building creative muscle

Another way to build creative muscle and access your creative self is to start a *training* program, by doing one small creative act a day. One mark, one image, one word a day will allow you to feel more alive.

Expressing your creativity daily is just as vital as breathing and eating. When you express your creativity, your heart becomes more joyous, a smile arises, and stress disappears.

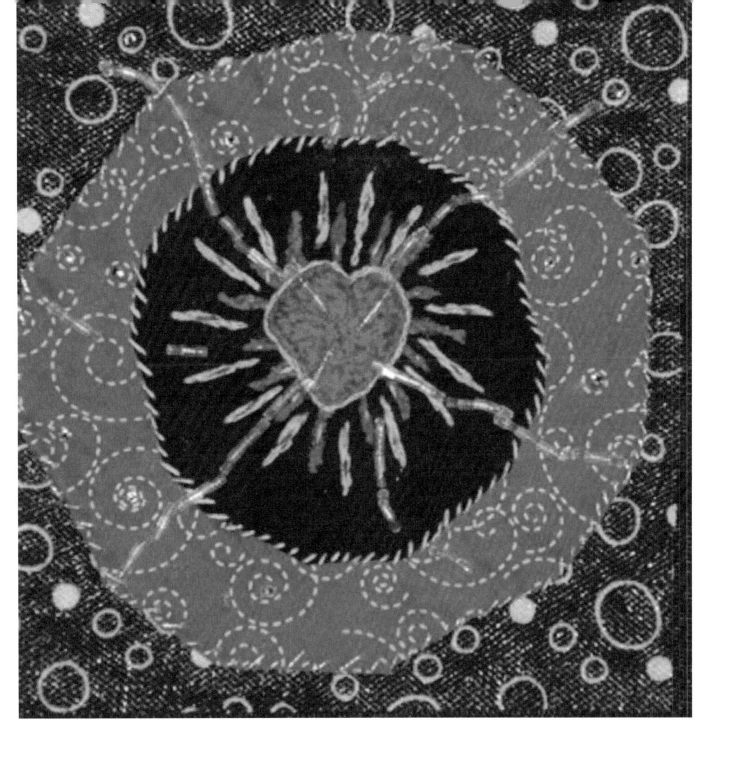

The invitation is for you to commit to one minute or more to creativity each day. I know you can do this no matter how busy you are. You just need to say *yes*!

CREATE

MUSCLE MEMORY

Choose the medium you will work in. Remember, this is a daily practice, so it might be something you need to travel with.

Some examples are: a journal, paper, a drawing tablet (such as smartphone or iPad), a drum, a Ukulele, cardboard for collage, something to knit, needlepoint, or sew. Type, sculpt, dance, make music — by all means, choose what makes you happy.

But here's the thing:

- Work on only one project.

- Add to it everyday.

- You can layer over what you did the day before, don't remove anything or cover anything up because you don't like it.

As always, this is about the creative *process*, not the end result. Let your intuition guide you. There is no right or wrong, just the experience. If you get stuck, look at the Quick References section to see if you can unstick yourself. Happy creative-intuitive muscle building!

For deep revelations and healing, **trust the brush**.

Inviting parts of yourself to come back

The more you release old stuck beliefs about yourself, the more energy comes back to you in the form of your life force. There is a powerful healing therapy in shamanism, called Soul Retrieval, that returns fragmented parts of yourself back to you. Soul Retrieval brings your life force back into you.

You have heard the expression *being beside yourself*; in that moment, part of you is outside of yourself. It's a reactionary defense mechanism that provides *safety* for your *bodymindspirit*. For example, you are driving merrily, when suddenly you realize that you are about to get rear-ended. In that fraction of a second, the last thing you want to do is be in your body at the point of impact ... so part of your being leaves or dissociates for a split second, and then returns when it's safe enough to come back into your body. What happens when it never feels quite safe enough to come back? There are many reasons why parts of you don't fully come back to wholeness. For example, if you grew up in an emotionally violent household, perhaps you only had enough of your soul energy present to survive. When your life force is not whole, you survive with only partial life force. When you can be fully in your body you can do more than survive. You can thrive.

Here's another example of not being fully in your body. You have a lot on your mind, and you put the milk in the cupboard instead if the fridge. This is a momentary out-of-body experience. When you are fully present, you find the milk there and say, "How did that happen?" This is not a soul loss moment; it is an out-of-body moment. You are safe, and *all of you* comes back in a few minutes. Unless, of course, you do this often. Then you need to ask what keeps you from being fully present? Let the creative process show you the way back — fully into your body again.

The intuitive process, with the help of your wise inner muse creates little safety nets, small steps in healing your past memories so that you can start the journey to come home fully. With each brushstroke, you call your soul parts back from the shadow spaces where they feel safe, to honor them, and welcome them home into your heart.

7

Outside of the Box, Creative Warm-Ups

Okay, you have been reading for some time. Are you ready to do something creative? This chapter contains a series of *let-go* and *let-loose* exercises, to free your mind and body, to loosen your tight limits, and to invite your inner four-year-old to *play*!

Calling all four-year-olds

Crayons are the perfect way to invite your inner four-year-old to play. You most likely explored with color, an image, or a shape in coloring books as a young child. Coloring books gave you an *official* place to express your creative self. I think it would have been better if we had been given blank paper or even shapes and crayons to explore our creative muse. The lines in coloring books kept us in line, brought us into order, and taught us how to obey the rules and regulations of society. Lines and pre-made shapes told us how scenes *should* look, and the colors that should be used. They confined and restricted our expansive young selves.

Coloring books first made their appearance in the 1880s with Little Folks coloring books. In the 1950s, the introduction of the sixty-four

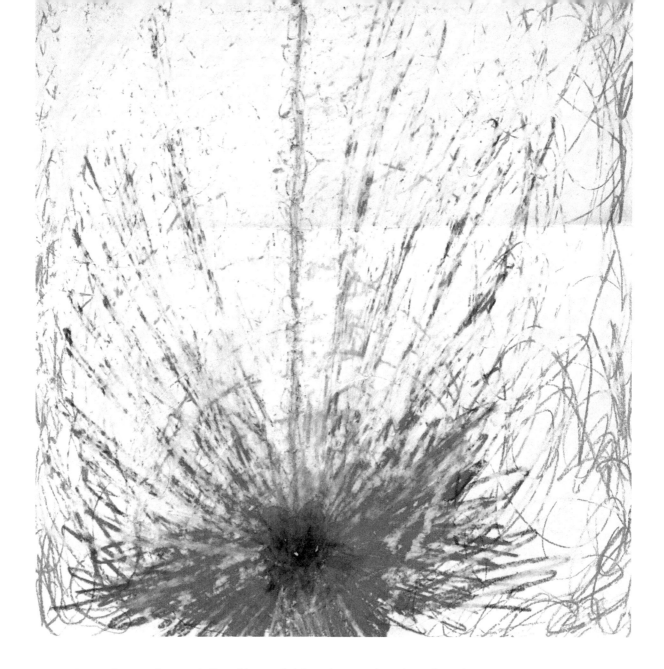

count box of Crayola's redefined how children learned and explored colors, images, and shapes. The box of named and premixed colors helped children name colors, but it limited creative exploration of colors as well. Just like using words to express something, once you name a color you limit the exploration of it.

For most of us, crayons were the first visually creative expressive tool we used. They are neat, accessible, and the most memory-inducing creative tool. If you close your eyes and imagine the smell of a crayon, chances are you can recall the smell and a memory of using them.

CREATE

PLAYING WITH CRAYONS ONE

Take out a plain sheet of paper, any size that calls to you. It can be a paper bag, newspaper, sketch book, or your journal.

For this exercise, I will ask you to close your eyes and invite your inner four-year-old to come out and play. You will doodle, make marks on paper, warm up your body to move, and encourage your mind to free up and play, and your soul to expand.

1. Grab a handful of crayons and any kind of paper— newspaper, shopping circulators, old magazines, and/or paper bags.

2. Now pick four or six colors that catch your eye.

3. Hold the crayons in both hands.

4. Close your eyes. Invite all your senses to open up.

5. Keep your eyes closed and make marks on your paper.

6. *Feel* the movement of your hand. *Smell* the wax of the crayons (savor the memories that the smell can bring up). *Hear* the sound of crayon against the paper. *Imagine* what it might look like (no peeking). *Notice* how your body, your mind, and your heart feel as you bring your inner four-year-old out to play.

CREATE

PLAYING WITH CRAYONS TWO

Have a few crayons in each hand. This time let your nondominant hand lead the movement and let your dominant hand follow. You may keep your eyes open or closed. Invite all your senses to wake up and feel the experience.

This exercise is a good way to balance the left and right sections of your brain, which engages both your logical and your creative neural pathways at the same time. Now, follow the new unfamiliar pattern that your nondominant hand is leading. Basically, it shakes things up.

When you complete this exercise, do a quick *body scan*. Notice what specific parts of your body *feel* different. Remember: no judgment, just notice.

Get Messy

When was the last time you finger-painted? Felt the paint squishing through your fingers? Or even toes? Now is the time to try it out.

First, let's get ready. Take some full, deep belly breaths. Breathe in from your nose. Trace your breath as it goes from your nose, to your throat, down your chest, into your belly. Feel your belly expand. Count to five. Then exhale. Following your breath out of your body—from belly, to chest, to throat, and out your mouth. Now you are in a centered place, a place of *intuition* rather than rational thinking.

CREATE

FINGER PAINTING

Dip your fingers into a paint color that is calling you, and engage all your senses. Feel where the paint on your fingers meets the paper. Does it make a sound?

Is there a smell to the paint? How does your body feel as you finger-paint? Alive, silly, awkward, curious, bored, awed, in a hurry?

Enjoy your body sensations; spend time just letting yourself be moved by the paint on paper for a while. Don't judge it. Really— don't judge it. You are warming up your body and mind to create and explore. Your spirit is already excited at the possibly. Play, explore, and expand with paint to paper.

I feel, therefore I create: Emotional croquis

In French, *croquis* means quick sketches, drawings that are quick expressions of a shape and energy, not necessarily a likeness. They will help you stay out of your rational mind and focus on what you presently feel. Respond to what you see and feel without worrying about right or wrong, perfect or ugly—raw or refined.

Just respond.

CREATE

FEEL AND RESPOND

Copy each word below onto separate pieces of paper then put them in a bowl.

Set up your creative space.

- Get grounded and balanced with your breath. When you are ready, pull a card from the bowl and *respond* to the word with color, shape, and form.

- Respond on paper for about a minute, and pull another and respond, using the same sheet of paper.

Another way of warming up your emotions and creative self is to make an audio recording of the emotions as you pull them out of the bowl. Give yourself three minutes between each word. When you are ready, play it, hear, feel, and *respond.* (To shake up the order of the words, shuffle the recording.)

Here are some emotion words. Add any words that move you to your own list.

Happy	Open	Alive	Quirky	Forgetful	Silly
Joyful	Interested	Curious	Excited	Forgiving	Regretful
Love	Powerful	Depressed	Anxious	Thankful	Upset
Confused	Indifferent	Afraid	Nervous	Gracious	Lonely
Fragmented	Angry	Scared	Faithful	Abandoned	Outraged
Small	Grateful	Hopeful	Peaceful	Faithful	Numb
Sad	Shame	Guilty	Furious	Bubbly	Sensual
Terrified	Alone	Irritated	Rejected	Obnoxious	Bitter

Color query

Colors evoke emotional reactions. Your body responds to and resonates with the vibration of color in nature, on fabric, a wall covering, and on another's face. Colors can elicit memories and powerful emotions, create movement in your body, and even heal.

This exercise is an opportunity to explore how your *bodymindspirit* reacts and responds to raw color — without a story and without your mind telling you how to react. Stay out of your rational mind and respond to what is in front of you. Respond to what you see and feel — without worrying about right or wrong, perfect or ugly, raw or refined.

Just. Respond.

CREATE
COLOR AND RESPOND

There are two ways do this color exercise.

- The first way is to write the words of the colors below onto separate bits of paper, and then put them in a bowl. The second way is to paint a small amount of each color on separate pieces of paper; that way you will have a card with just color, not words. We respond differently to color versus the word for the color. *Try both ways.*

- Paint all your responses on the same sheet of paper. Pull a card and respond to each color with paint on paper for about a minute. Pull another card. Give yourself about a minute to respond to that color, then pull another.

Here are some colors to work with:

red	yellow	purple	light blue
black	orange	turquoise	green
gray	gold	magenta	brown
blue	silver	pink	white

Feel free to add any colors that you want.

Have fun.

A STORY

Taking risks and healing an old pattern

Standing in front of my painting, I asked it, "What do you want next?" I felt resistance to doing anything more to it. Why? Because I *liked* it. "Red" was the answer. Red? My MIND went nuts. Red did not *fit* into my painting!

I believe that all of the risks that we take during our creative explorations are *training wheels for life*. So, after my mental shock, I surveyed all my red options and picked up a large, fat, red, oil pastel and went for it. My mind was fighting for the first ten seconds—then I surrendered and experienced playfulness and joy.

Realizations that show up during an intuitive creative process are *metaphors for life learnings, for growth and change*. The experience of learning and understanding what shows up on paper will seep into your *bodymindspirit* muscle memory, your subtle energy fields, and start to transform your life, from the inside to the outside.

An example: For years, all the reasons I can't *be X* have been showing up in my paintings. What showed up was shame, self-hatred, fear, avoidances, not being smart enough, and all the countless (mostly unconscious) lies I told myself. All those years, I accepted my faults as my truth. I told myself lies, including "I can't write." During the restorative healing of myself, through paint and paper, I acknowledge the delicate, fragile, scared parts of myself along with the kick-ass-I-can-do-anything persona. All of this gave me the courage to write this book.

Now, I honor those moments of courage, those tiny moments of going for it! Streaming out into my day-to-day life, they are new opportunities for exploration and growth.

Make an ugly painting: Go ahead Get it out of your system

Let's start acknowledging your biggest fears: What if I mess this painting up? What if I don't like it? Your mantra, chant, prayer will be *Process*, not *Product*. What is important is what you learn about yourself, not what it looks like.

So ...

Here is your opportunity to make the ugliest painting you can make. Don't even think about skipping this exercise. It is important. The fear of not doing something right, in this case, ugly, not perfect, can stop you from living fully.

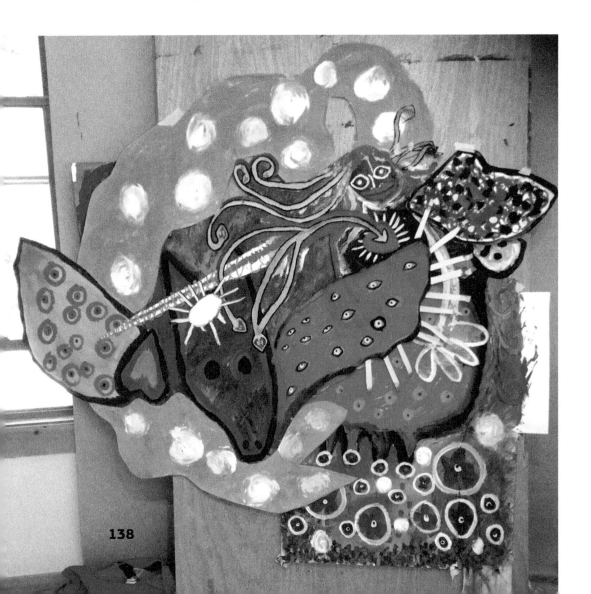

CREATE

MAKE IT UGLY

Set up your painting space. Ground yourself.
Ask for a foundation blessing.

So make an ugly painting. Invite all that hidden ugliness to show up and come out of you via paint on paper. Use a brush, your hands, and other things to make marks. Go ahead. Scratch away at the paint. Throw paint. Don't tear it up.

Just keep moving.

Try not to step back and look—that will engage your mind. You want a mind-free, judgment-free zone.

Just keep moving, and if sounds want to come out, let them. Don't hold back. After all, it is just kids' paint on paper.

Keep painting ... just keep painting ... just keep painting ...

Heart art

An art bud of mine, Corrine Gillman, created this exploration. I love it and I had to share it. This can be a simple creative exercise you can do everyday.

CREATE

SPREAD THE LOVE

Set up your painting space. Ground yourself.
Ask for a foundation blessing.

• Paint your heart as you visualize it today.

• Tomorrow make it bigger. Give yourself room to grow. Keep going, letting your heart spill out and get really big ... bigger ... biggest.

• Write words of love to your heart.

• Put yourself in your heart. Share secret dreams and wishes.

• Make this heart as beautiful as you are.

• Make one, make many. Start a heart journal to fill your life with hearts.

Creative Alchemy

Before enlightenment —
chop wood and carry water.
After enlightenment —
chop wood and carry water.

— A Zen Proverb

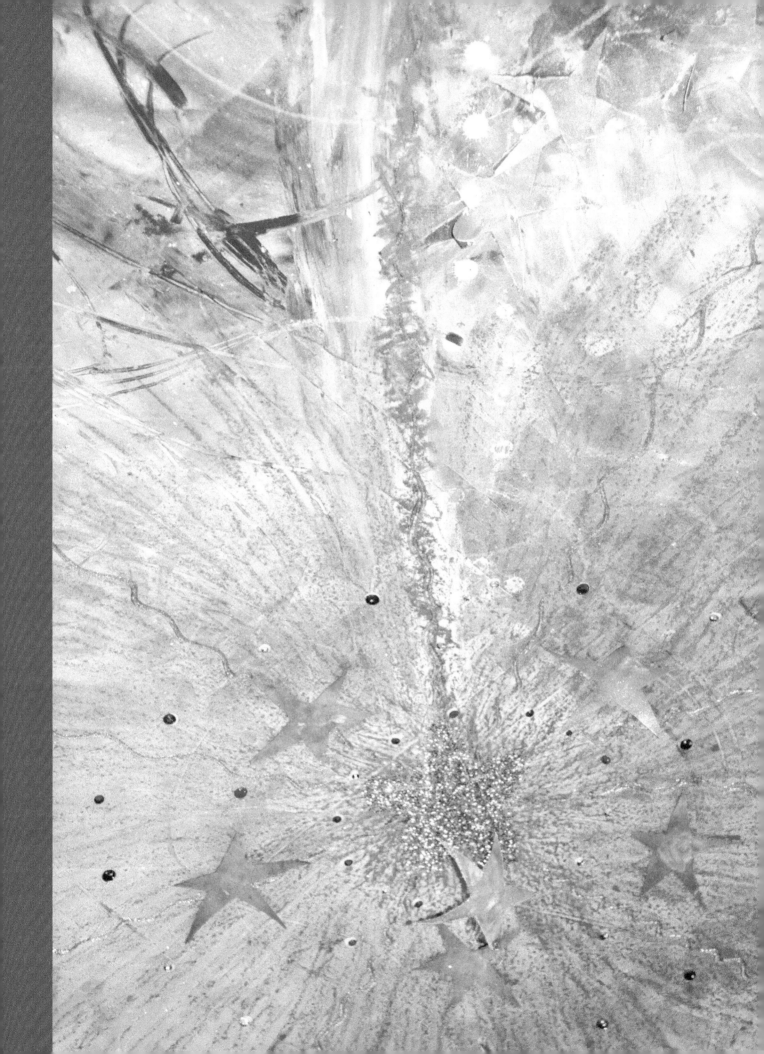

CHAPTER

8

Building Your Vibration

You are not alone. You'll have plenty of help to support your creative healing and strengthen your intuitive self. The exercises will guide you to the power of your true vibration. Here you can draw energy from the Elements, words, guardian energies, and heaven and earth.

The first thing I do when I am setting up for a painting session is to create sacred space, for myself or for the group I'm facilitating. Creating sacred space puts the ordinary world on hold for a few hours and invites you to step fully into the creative process. Creating sacred space allows your intuitive self, your feeling self, to come a bit more forward so you may start your inner dialogue with color, shape, and form.

ENERGY EXERCISE
Allowing yourself to arrive

Connect to your heart, to your breath, and to Heaven and Earth.

- First, ground yourself and become fully present to where you are at this moment.

- Feel the air move around you.

- Hear any sounds around you, and within you.

- Sit comfortably in a chair, on the floor, or on your couch.

- Close your eyes.

- Breathe in and follow your breath into your body. How far does it go? To your chest? Diaphragm? Or all the way down, below your navel?

Now bring your awareness to where your body meets the Earth. If your feet are not actually touching the Earth, then this is the place where your body touches whatever you are sitting on that's resting on the Earth. Feel the weight of your body as the Earth supports it. Feel how you yield to the Earth and the Earth yields to you.

Allow your breath to travel down your body to the place where your body meets the Earth. Then let your body send roots down into the earth from this place — traveling down deep, grounding you, rooting you. Know that as your roots travel deep they also travel horizontally to stabilize you.

As you travel down to the molten core of the Earth, feel the love and warmth of Fire, the love of this planet, and wrap your toes/ roots around the core. Then breathe up that warmth and love from the Earth into you. Now, when your breath energy comes up from the Earth again, let it go all the way up to the crown of your head and keep traveling up to a center point above you. I use the Sun or the North Star as my heavenly center point.

The sun at it's highest point is the center of the day sky. The North Star is the center of the night sky. In Chinese mythology, our energy extends to the North Star. It extends from the top of our heads to the center of the sky, which allows us to receive divine wisdom. There is even an acupuncture point, Upper Star, which mirrors North Star energy, and it is said to hold the vibrational blueprint of who we are.

Let your breath, travel up to the North Star or Sun, connecting to that center point, and then bring your breath that is infused with heavenly love and warmth down into your body. The rhythm is up to you. I recommend at least three breath/energy exchanges to the Earth's energy below and the Heaven's energy above. When you feel centered and calm, bring your awareness to your chest and your heart area. Bring your hands up in prayer position at your heart level and take a bow to yourself, honoring yourself.

This is a great exercise to do daily, to center and prepare yourself for your creative time or your everyday routine.

Making your Space Sacred: Welcoming in the Elements

Lighting a candle and smudging your space will make your creative womb sacred. In addition you can welcome in the Web of Life: The Land and the Elements around you. Since this is an intuitive creative process, I encourage you to follow your heart, and create a ritual that feels right for you.

I light a candle signaling that I am opening sacred space. Candlelight reminds us that we all have the light of love in our hearts. I like to engage all of my senses and then smudge with incense, sage, or essential oils (rose or orange). Lighting a candle and changing the scent of the room triggers your body, mind, and spirit that you have entered a special time.

I then like to acknowledge the Four Directions (North, East, South, West) and the Four Elements (Air, Fire, Water, Earth). Different traditions use different colors, directions, and associations for each direction. This is your creative space, so do whatever intuitively feels right. Take back your power and your knowing. Try not to let your mind get in the way by insisting that you follow one tradition or another— instead, create your own. Part of living authentically is honoring what feels right for you.

In my heart or out loud I say something like this:

> *Welcome in the direction of East, the energy of birth and change. May this energy bring forth creative possibilities.*
>
> *Welcome in the direction of South, the energy of excitment, passion, and gratitude. May this energy bring forth creative passion.*
>
> *Welcome in the direction of West, the energy of yielding and clarity. May this energy bring forth creative discernment.*
>
> *Welcome in the direction of North, the energy of fluidity and deep listening. May this energy bring forth creative insights.*

COMMON ASSOCIATIONS FOR THE FOUR DIRECTIONS

(Northern Hemisphere orientation)

EAST	SOUTH	WEST	NORTH
Spring	Summer	Autumn	Winter
Birth	Flower	Harvest	Seed
Sunrise	High sun	Sunset	Moonrise
Vision	Heart centered	Inspiration	Wisdom
Creative	Community	Letting go	Learning
Where you are going	Zenith	Distillation	Where you came from
Sap rising	Maturation	Harvest/pruning	Hibernation
Idea	Sharing	Decreasing	Condensing
Add your own	Add your own	Add your own	Add your own

I also like to welcome the energy Below that supports us, and the energy Above that inspires us, because without them we would not be on this beautiful planet and in this beautiful body.

May all beings be happy and may your intuitive creative heart lead you to new discoveries of your magnificent self.

The Elements: The combined gifts of the Elements (Fire, Air, Earth, Water) is what gives us our beautiful body. Again, do what feels right for you. Many cultures have traditions of honoring the Elements, for instance, Southeast Asian Water Festival, Beltane Fire Festival, Morning Sun songs, Earth Day. I also like to welcome in the Elemental energy.

Welcome Water—which holds us in its energy as we gestate in our mother's womb. Fluidity.

Welcome Air—the first to greet us when we are born, the last to leave us when we die. Air constantly infuses us with life force, allowing us to let go of what is no longer needed. Changeability.

Welcome Fire—our heart, our blood, the pulse and rhythm of our life. Passion.

Welcome Earth—our bones, our flesh and our body. Grounded-ness.

Say anything else that is in your heart—your intentions, dreams, and prayers. Now your space is sacred, set apart from and out of time.

Blessing words

Words are powerful. Words are healing. Words can also be destructive and used as weapons. Being mindful of what we say or even think about ourselves and others is vital to our individual health and health of the whole world. Would you rather put out toxic words of hate and fear or words of love and healing?

When we intuitively create, we try not to use words (unless words are your creative medium) because words can limit our experience. Using a word instead of a color, shape, or form, makes an experience seem finite instead of infinite.

The blessing words that you will bring forth for this exercise are your *power words*: intentional words that will create the foundation for your painting.

We have created a sacred space, a nurturing womb for your creativity. We have acknowledged the Four Elements and Four Directions.

Foundational blessing

Now close your eyes and ask your intuitive self for two or three words — a dedication, which will set the foundation of your painting. Take the first words that come to you. Don't censor them; they do not need to make sense. For example — whole, green, circle, bored. Once you get your first words, write them on your paper with a pencil. The words will get covered up as you paint, but the blessing and foundation will remain.

The Pregnant Void

Often a void is thought of as an empty vacuum, a place where nothing exists. I invite you to imagine the Void, the pregnant Void, as the place where all growth, life, and expression starts and is birthed from.

Take a moment and focus your intention to experience the vibration of the pregnant Void, the womb of all existence that is alive and vibrating inside each of your cells.

CREATE

POTENTIALITY

Set up your supplies and creative space.

Close your eyes. Take a deep breath in, and ground yourself.
Ask for a foundation blessing and write those on your paper,
or hold them in your heart.

Let your mind relax and be open to all possibilities.

- Now bring your awareness from your belly to your
  heart space. Feel the space around your heart expand.

- With each breath, allow yourself to go deeper and
  deeper into your heart space. Ask to experience the
  vibration of the pregnant Void that resides in your
  heart space.

- Bring all your senses to experience that vibration: what
  do you hear, feel, smell, see?

- Let that vibration of the pregnant Void fill you
  and awaken the pregnant possibilities in your
  bodymindspirit.

- Ask your intuitive creative self to express the vibration
  of the pregnant Void inside with color, shape, and form.

- Let the energy flow—don't judge it or restrain it. Let
  the fullness of the Void in you come forth with paint
  onto paper.

- As you paint, how you feel? Do you feel more alive? Full
  of potentiality?

Meet your true self

Vitality, energy, and vibration came in with you as you entered this body. Each cells holds the truth of who you are. Way before the pink and blue conversation — before the social *should haves* kicked in, there was — and still is — a *pure true* vibration of you. This pure vibration is your soul's life force. Your true self.

One of the most powerful healing aspects of this creative process is that the more you paint, the more the truth of who you are comes forth. The intuitive creative process removes many layers (limiting beliefs) that cloud your true self vibration. The physical movement

of painting wakes up the memory of your true self in all your *body-mindspirit* cells. This memory resonates and aligns with your pure true energy. The more you paint, the more that memory of your pure true vibration comes forth.

As you set up your creative womb, hold the intention in your heart to paint with the energy and vibration of your true self, and to experi-ance your true self with all your senses. Remember that your intuitive self will show you only what you are ready for. Part of the healing aspect of this intuitive creative process is that your body and spirit will remember the experience of *this* core vibration and change in your *bodymindspirit* muscle memory. So, don't worry. Your being will remember much more than your memory will recall when you are fin-ished painting.

So go ahead. It's time to remember this pure true part of yourself.

CREATE

TRUE-SELF VIBRATION, PAINT IT FORTH

Set up your supplies and creative space.

Close your eyes. Take a deep breath in, and ground yourself. Welcome in the Elements and your guides. Ask for a foundation blessing and write those on your paper, or hold them in your heart.

- Ask to feel the vibration of your true self. The *vibration* may start as a tingling feeling in your heart. Let that energy grow and expand out from your heart area, let it fill your torso, your chakras, and then move out to your whole body.

- Let the vibrating energy expand into the energy surrounding your body, into your auric fields.

- Feel that energy move out into the world, meeting other true vibrations — vibrations of plants, minerals, animals, Air, Fire, Water, Earth, and even other humans.

- Notice how you meet-merge-exchange energy, but ultimately you remain wholly yourself.

- Now that your true-self vibration is awakened, go and paint. With the help of your creative muse, reawaken that vibration through color, shape, and form.

Part of the painting process is to expand — and sometimes part of the painting process is to illustrate your roadblocks. Keep painting. Enjoy bringing forth your true self energy again and again.

Meet your soul group

Have you noticed that you tend to meet and socialize with folks
who have similar interests and outlooks on life and the world?
Imagine that we originate from a group of souls with the same
energy, understanding, gifts, and vibrations. When our soul
chooses to be born into human form and come to earth, we tend
to seek those like-minded human beings to share our life with.

Each of us belongs to a soul group or soul family and
their purpose are to provide loving support and also
to help us to learn our life lessons!

—Sarah K Sherphaerg

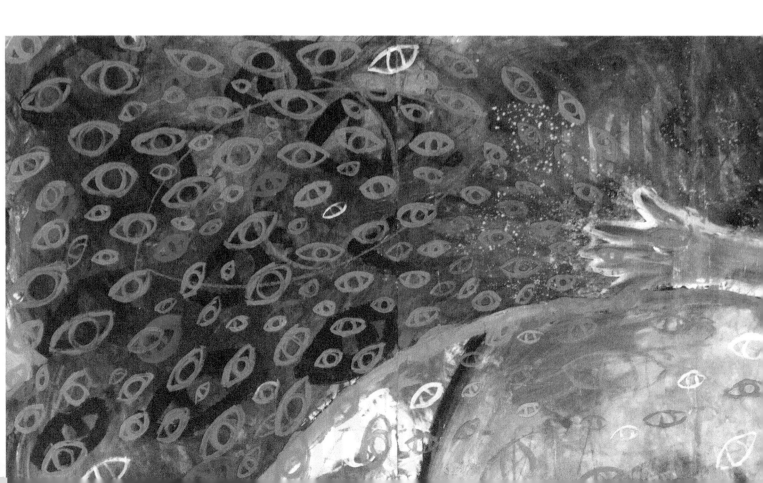

CREATE

CONNECT WITH YOUR ORIGINAL CLAN

Set up your creative space and womb.

Close your eyes. Take a deep breath in, and ground yourself.

Ask for a foundation blessing and write those on your paper, or hold them in your heart.

- Quiet yourself with your breath. Notice your breathing rhythm. Your heartbeat. The flow of your blood. Then bring your awareness to that still place in your heart, that's so full of potential—your heart space, that knows your soul group, and the vibrations of your soul group.

- Feel your core energy stirring and becoming more and more accessible for you as you bring your awareness toward the vibration of your Soul group.

- Ask to be shown the energy and vibration of your soul group through color, shape, and form, using your intuitive, creative self as an intermediary.

- Take your time—listen and respond.

- Some of the vibration will feel familiar and some will be new. Take it all in.

- Notice how you feel when you paint and move with this energy. Let your soul vibration wake up your soul cell memories and infuse your being with your soul group vibration.

Meet your guardian energies

Shamanic cultures believe that we are born with guardian energies around us. These guardian energies give us guidance and protection. They can be in human form, animal form, or a mix (think of Greek mythology — human heads with animal bodies). We still have guardian spirits around us, although they may be viewed differently or not be considered as important and mainstream as they were in the past.

If guardian helping spirits were not part of your childhood story, perhaps your family spoke to you about your guardian angels. Perhaps you had a special stuffed animal that you could not allow out of your sight, because you believed it kept you safe.

You don't always have a name for these protective energies, but you can feel them—they make you feel safer, calmer, braver, more protected. When they are with you, you feel safer, calmer, braver, more protected. The imaginary friend you had as child, most likely was your helping spirit/your guardian angel. Indigenous peoples believe that in addition to our guardian spirit we also have helping *animal* spirits — sometimes called power animals or totem animals. They too, are around to protect you, or to help you with a particular part of your life.

There are many ways to access the wisdom of your healing spirits: automatic writing, shamanic journeying, and intuitive creative acts.

Our helping spirits always have a higher perspective than we do, because they are not confined to an earthly form. They are here to help us with our earthly walk, to guide and protect us.

Some cultures teach their young ones how to cultivate relationships with their helping spirits from the start. Who says we don't believe in helping spirits in our modern culture? Even today when a child is born, our community brings gifts of stuffed animals (power animals) and rattles (to help connect with our guardian sprits and the Web of Life). Both are traditional gifts for a child to build power and give protection. If this was not part of your family upbringing, it does not mean that your helping spirits have left you. Your helping sprits are always around watching over you, whether you are aware of them or not. I love the bumper sticker that reminds us that our helping spirits are always around: "Never drive faster that your angel can fly!"

What was your favorite stuffed animal when you were young? Do you remember your imaginary friend? What images did you fill your room with as a child: animals, rainbows, nature? Think about the age before superheroes and rock stars, which have their own resonant archetypal energy inside you.

Now let's create a space to meet the energy of your helping spirits. Remember that your intuitive creative self will speak to you in color, shape, and form. Feel the connection as you become reacquainted with your guardian energies. Don't try to direct knowing or to make it look like what your rational mind thinks it should. Allow the energy and vibration of your helping spirits to come through with paint onto paper. Recalling this energy is essential in your *bodymindspirit* cellular memory; it allows all of you to wake up and remember that protective, wise, helping energy in you and around you.

Over time new helping spirits may join you, to guide you in different aspects in your life. You can have one, two or a whole council of helping spirits at any time.

What guardian wants to come forth to defend your **soul's truth** and your heart?

CREATE

MEET THE VIBRATION OF YOUR HELPING SPIRIT IN HUMAN(ISH) FORM

Remember that the visions in our subconscious are free form, not constrained. Angels may not have wings and be angelic, just like horses can have human heads. Be open to the unexpected.

As you set up your creative womb, in your heart hold an invitation to meet the energy of your guardian angel. Ask your guardain to speak to you with color, shape, and form.

Light a candle. Take some deep breaths. Set up your painting space. Create your sacred space. Ground yourself.

Are there any blessing words that rise up to be placed on the paper? If so, write them on the paper now.

Now, bring your awareness to your heart area. Feel your breath moving into your heart.

- Feel your request to meet the energy of your guardian spirit stirring in your heart.

- Feel that energy moving out to your limbs, enlivening your entire being.

- Now look at your paints. Pick up the color(s) that calls to you. It might appear brighter than the rest or pull you like a magnet. Make the first mark on the paper — then the next mark — and the next mark …

- Let the energy of your guardian angel fill you and reawaken that vibration in you as you paint. Follow the energy! Trust the brush! Trust your heart!

CREATE
MEET YOUR POWER ANIMAL

Set up the painting space, just as you did when you wanted to meet your guardian angel energy.

Ground yourself.

Are there any blessing words that rise up to be placed on the paper? If so, write them on the paper now.

- Allow your heart's intention to "Meet your power animal".

- Feel that energy vibration move through your heart, through your whole body until you feel that knowing, perhaps like an ancient memory.

- Let that energy rise and fill you up. Allow that energy to speak to you via color, shape, and form.

- Be open to the possibility that your visual represen-tation of your power animal may not even look like an animal. It is all about the vibration of your power animal in your *bodymindspirit*, not what it looks like!

- Open your heart to the experience and deep knowing. Paint whatever wants to shows up. Don't direct it or guide it.

The learnings, knowings, and experiences you have as you paint are more important than the painting outcome. Your heart knows what animal energy it is. Often shamanic animals don't look like ones you see in this world. Often they are a fusion of different critters all in one. You know in your heart the name of that animal — Ant, Crow, Moose, Whale, or maybe just Fuzzy.

As with every painting in this book — allow the energy to be different than you expect. Why limit yourself?

Creating a vibrational painting of your helping spirits is a wonderful way to honor them. Another way to honor and build relationships with your helping spirits is to have something that represents them in your everyday life: a photograph, a piece of jewelry, a statue, for example. You will be surprised that once you reconnect with your helping spirits' energies, you will feel them all around you.

Once you remember that you are part of the Web of Life, part of the Spirit That Lives In All Things, your guardian spirits will reflect that spirit-filled aspect of yourself back to you, always showing you your truth.

An Elemental meeting

Everything is alive and has spirit. Water is alive and has spirit, and so does Air, Sun, Grass, Soil, and Sky. Somehow, in our *modern* society we have forgotten about our relationship with the Elements, and we take them for granted. We think we have evolved and don't need to relate to the Elements; but we still need the Earth under our feet, Air to breathe, Water to sustain us, and Fire to warm us. We are created from and formed by the Elements. We live in Water for the first nine months of our lives in the womb. At birth, we are greeted by Air. Earth is our body, and Fire is our spirit. We *are* the Elements. We are part of the Web of Life.

CREATE

GREETING FIRE, AIR, WATER, EARTH

The intention for this creative exploration is to see, feel, and experience each Element as you relate to it. Find the gift and vibration that you and this Element share, and bring that forth in a creative act. This is shamanic art. It's the gift of the power of your relationship with the Elements.

Set up your painting space. Create your sacred space. Ground yourself. Ask for a foundation blessing.

- Take some deep breaths in and allow your heart space to open.

- Decide which Element (Fire, Air, Water, Earth) you want to meet via color, shape, and form.

- Stand in front of your paper, close your eyes, and invite in the Element that you decide to work with today. Let that Elemental energy fill your whole body, and let your body move with that Elemental expression.

- When you are ready, open your eyes and choose the first color that stands out. Let the Elemental energy inside you speak to you with color, shape, and form.

- You may do one painting for each Element, or combine them onto one creative work. Do whatever feels right to you.

This creative act is an honoring to the Elements that give you life. A powerful creation that represents the Elemental energy inside you.

The One becomes two.

The two becomes three.

The three becomes 10,000 things.

—Lao Tzu: The Tao Te Ching

Meeting Above and Below in you

As humans we stand between Heaven and Earth, receiving both the gifts and support from Above and Below. In this creative exploration, I invite you to explore the Above (Heavenly energy) and the Below (Earthly energy) in you.

The Great One divides becoming Heaven (energy) and Earth (flesh/bones).

CREATE

EARTH AND HEAVEN

Set up your creative womb.

Close your eyes. Take a deep breath in, and ground yourself.

Welcome in the Elements and your guides.

Ask for a foundation blessing and write those on your paper, or hold them in your heart.

- As you stand between Heaven and Earth — Above and Below invite that energy to be present in you, to move through you and express its vibration via color, shape, and form.

- Allow your intuitive self to guide this vibration and manifest the beauty of your Heaven on Earth onto paper.

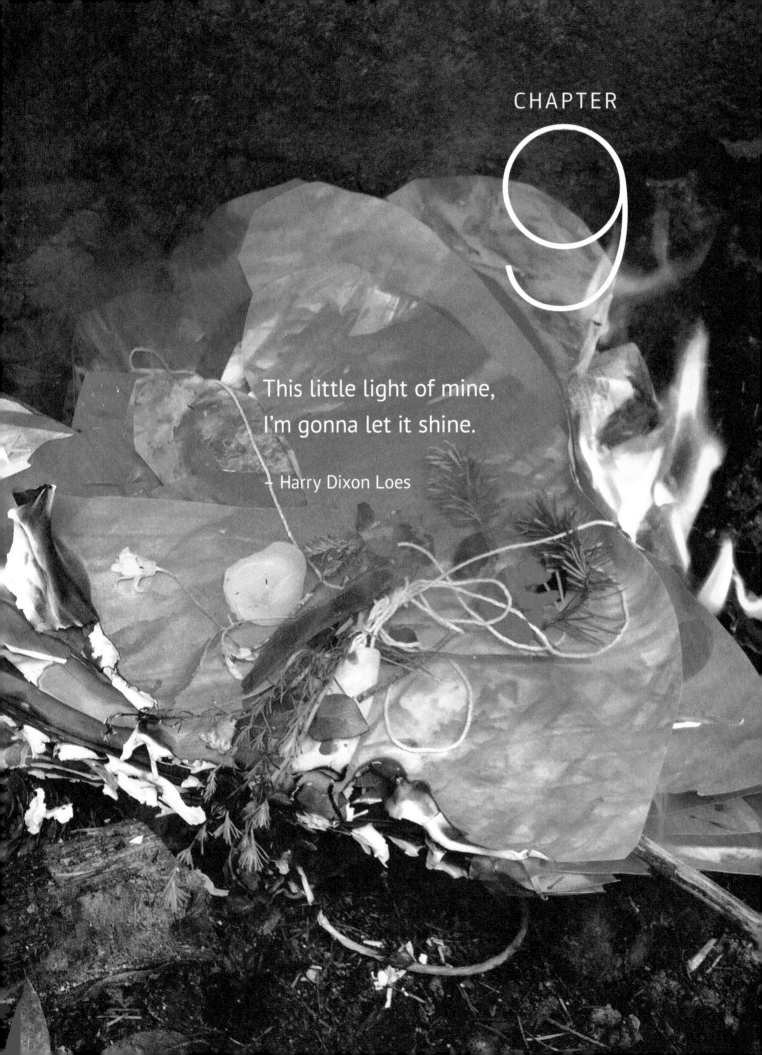

This little light of mine,
I'm gonna let it shine.

– Harry Dixon Loes

Be Brave—
Releasing What Is
in the Way

If you are afraid of an alligator under your bed, you might discover that it's a friendly alligator—a creature who just wants to help you become more fully yourself. Or it might simply be a forgotten sweater. Your intutive creation can transform what's in the way of your vitality.

Creative healing

One of many things the intuitive creative process can show you is what is keeping you from being fully present in the world. It is essential to look at those bumps, blocks, and stories that hold you back from growing, changing, and shining your light.

Creative healing happens when you shine a little light and demystify those blocks, paint them; allowing the creative process to help move and integrate that life force back into your body. The good news is you don't have to rip the Band-Aid off an old wound over and over again or tear down your entire defense system to bring back all the various parts of yourself. All you need to do is allow and trust your inner creative self to be your guide.

Letting your intuitive self lead the way, you can explore a belief pattern that is ready for change at a pace that is comfortable for you. When you mix the intuitive creative act with attention, curiosity, and acceptance to unblock old stories (speed bumps), healing can happen.

Here is an example: As a child you had a spot in your room that was dark; your mind made up all kinds of scary stories about it. Then one day the light shone in that area, and you realized it was just like the rest of your walls and floors. Or you got brave enough to shine a flashlight in the area (during the day of course), and what you feared was no longer scary.

Perhaps some really scary things have shown up in your life. Maybe you are afraid to look at them, or you simply want them to go away. The beauty of letting your intuitive self be the guide is that your dark, scary places show up only when you are ready, and always in little chunks that you are capable of processing and integrating. Allowing a little light into those places brings awareness and healing. I call this *creative alchemy*.

Invite your creative muse to bring light to the shadow parts of yourself. Light and awareness lets you transform and integrate those hidden parts of yourself, creating wholeness. Consciously or unconsciously, you recognize aspects of your shadow self, and, as you recognize and accept those shadow parts, they are transformed from dark, heavy, and dense to light and true.

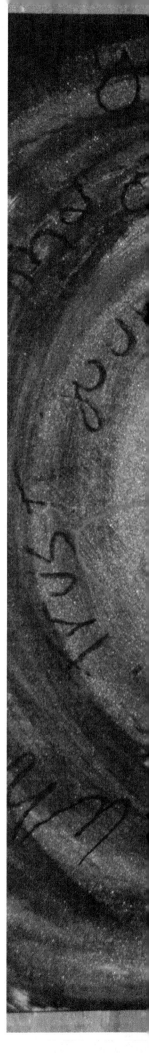

> **Alchemy — the act of transforming base dense ideas/matter into light/gold.**

Our energy body holds a blueprint that our physical body mimics. As we follow our intuitive creative self, we clear those old holding patterns and release blocks. The result is that our physical body rebalances, bringing lightness to who we are, remembering our true-self vibration. With each discovery, we change our dense old body vibration and embody our true, higher, brighter vibration. It feels natural and right when we come home to ourselves.

Under all the layers of expectations and self-impositions is a fully alive, unique you waiting to come home.

Meet your shadow self

One of the most profound gifts of this work is the opportunity to look at and explore parts of yourself that you usually are afraid to acknowledge. When we don't look at those parts, they tend to leak out unregulated, and can look like: hysterical crying, flying-off-the-handle rage, sinking to the depths of depression, being a bit too pissy, over-controlling, overly accommodating, or way too polite.

Going back to what we have explored, your shadow self consists of those parts of yourself you have put away, because you don't want other folks to see them. It is often our young self that labeled that part bad. Now as your adult self, it is time to reclaim all of your parts. Let's go a step further and deeper.

Have you put away:

- A strong part?

- A magical part?

- A sweet, soft part of you?

- The part of you that says *"NO"* and means it?

- The brutally honest part of you?

- The part of you that is just too big, loud, or "out there"?

Your intuition will show you the one part of you that wants to be a conscious part of you again. That part needs the most healing at this moment. That part is ready to be seen and brought back into the fold of your everyday self.

CREATE

RECOVERING PARTS FROM THE DARK

Set up your space. Close your eyes. Take a deep breath in, and ground yourself. Welcome in the Elements and your guides. Ask for a foundation blessing and write those on your paper, or hold them in your heart.

Sit for a few minutes in front of your paper. Know in your heart that you will be calling back a part of you that has been hidden away in your shadow place because you didn't feel safe enough to show that part to the world. Your intuitive creative self knows the shadow part that is ready to join you. Trust.

- Close your eyes and breathe into the sweet spot in your heart area.

- Feel your breath moving in and out of you.

- Feel your heartbeat.

- Feel the place where your body meets the earth.

- Feel yourself being supported by the earth.

- Now ask your all-knowing intuitive self for a color, shape, or form that will start a conversation to welcome back an essential part of you.

- Pick up your brush and follow the energy.

With one brushstroke at a time, creative alchemy happens. Your intuitive self will lead the way to a more integrated you.

A Ceremony for the Saboteur

Critic, saboteur, your mind—are all names for the energy that side-tracks you or completely distracts you from the matters at hand. There are a multitude of reasons why this energy exists in your life, but mostly it's to keep you safe. This energy is part of you, just like the bright, shiny, happy parts that you show the world. Like all other parts of you, this energy must be accepted for you to live as an authentic whole person. That also includes the potentially bratty, grumpy, snippy parts of you. To ignore those denser shadowy parts of yourself is like not recognizing the left side of your body.

Are you ready to meet your critic/saboteur and love her/him fully? Bring the invisible to form: Write a physical description of your critic/saboteur, including things like what it looks like, is wearing, what she/

If you hear a voice within you say 'you cannot paint,' then by all means paint, and that voice will be silenced.

– Vincent van Gogh

he/it often says to you. Be as detailed as possible. Create an image of your critic/saboteur. Invite the energy of your critic/saboteur to speak to you via color, shape, and form. Don't direct the dialogue. Let your wise, intuitive self be the intermediary.

Bringing the critic/saboteur into form can help you have a better understanding of energy that holds you back and to recognize it when it overrides you.

Honoring your critic/saboteur is as vital as honoring the creative part of yourself. You may think that your critic would critique everything, and would not have a soft side. The critic is always trying to keep you from stepping into "unsafe" territory. It is always on high alert, which is an exhausting job. Inviting your critic to rest while you paint gives you more space for creative expression and gives your critic a rest, too. While you are in this intuitive creative womb, you are safe, safe to explore your inner worlds. You don't need your bodyguard (critic) with you. Tell it that you are safe and will be fine on your own for a while.

Let your critic/saboteur know it can join you again when you are done painting (if you want). Putting the critic away for a while and letting your defenses down for a bit allows you to see, receive, and experience the learnings that show up, without the defensive knee-jerk response that is often the critic's first reaction. To grow and change, you will need to give your critic a vacation, a leave of absence, or a new job, so that you are no longer being held back.

Honor thy critic

Imagine your critic/saboteur in full detail. Imagine a shelf high above your creative space. Then imagine a box filled with soft and beautiful things — things that your critic/saboteur would just love. Invite your critic/saboteur to go and rest in the box for a while. Think of it as a spa for your critic, a place it can rest and step away from its lifelong project of keeping you safe.

Take a deep breath and let your body relax. Feel the space in your body that the critic/ saboteur resides in. This may be one area of your body, several spots, or an overall layer around you. Acknowledge all of the hard work that your critic/saboteur has done for you — how it has kept you safe all these years. Tell your critic that you love it. Dance a dance of love, write a poem, sing a song to it, honor it.

Invite your critic to take a break, and name a length of time that feels right for you. Tell your critic/saboteur that you are much stronger and wiser than when it started protecting you. Imagine your critic/saboteur snuggling down into the box and falling asleep. How do you feel when that energy is sleeping? Just notice. All relationships are reciprocal. You might have needed the critic/saboteur as much as it thought it needed to protect you. Just notice.

Send your critic/saboteur lots of love. After all, it is part of you, and honoring all parts of you is essential to living a full authentic life.

Superhero

Fairy tales, superheroes, and heroine stories were ways for us, as children, to understand different types of people and situations. They taught us lessons of right, wrong, good, bad, courage, fear, and trust.

These stories taught you how to trust yourself, your community, and higher powers. If you were to be any superhero/ine or fairy-tale character, who would it be?

Take the first one that comes to you. Don't try to understand the why or the story that comes with that archetypal character.

What you create will not look like that character; you are bringing forth the vibrations of that archetype's energy. Invite the energy of that character to speak to you via color, shape, and form. Be open to every possibility that shows up. Don't limit yourself to a likeness. As you create, let your body move the way your superhero would move.

CREATE

EXPRESS YOUR SUPERHERO

Set up your space. Close your eyes. Take a deep breath in, and ground yourself. Welcome in the Elements and your guides. Ask for a foundation blessing and write those on your paper, or hold them in your heart.

- Think of an archetypal character whose vibration you would like to explore. Let the qualities of that character wake up those qualities inside yourself. Notice all of your body sensations.

- Now ask that character's energy what is the first color, shape, or form that wants to come forth?

- Start to paint.

- Keep following the lead of that character's energy that has awakened inside you.

- Ignore the story if one shows up. You can think about it when you are done painting.

- Just keep painting.

The colors, shapes, and forms that show up may not look like anything that you think is part of that character. That's okay! You are painting the energy, the vibration of that character filtered through the uniqueness of you. So let your superhero/ine, god/ dess, fairytale character appear on paper.

Remember we are myriad feelings, emotions, experiences, and they all come without judgment onto the paper.

Releasing fears

Being cautious keeps us safe, like the critic's role. Caution allows you to understand your boundaries: when to push, hold, or even retreat, if necessary. But when your caution escalates into fear and starts to create personal limitations, then the fear needs to be explored, understood, and sometimes, disarmed.

Let's paint your fears. *What! Paint what I'm afraid of!* Do you feel yourself retreating? Are you thinking *I'm out of here*?

But wait. Before you close the book, run out the door, and binge on chocolate bars, potato chips, or both, remember that your big-hearted, loving, intuitive self will guide you in the most delicate way. You will guide yourself to your greatest learning opportunity that is ready to emerge. You won't notice this understanding at first. It slides under the radar, in a language that only your subconscious understands. Then it overflows into your daydreams, your night dreams, and finally up to the level of your body and mind. Often these fears start to be disarmed in your dreams—then in your waking life as you explore them and paint them forth. Each brushstroke will change your *body-mindspirit* muscle memory from an old outdated holding pattern to a new, open, receptive, and integrated balance.

Desire urges me on, as fear bridles me.

– Giordano Bruno

CREATE

RELEASING FEARS

So ... be brave. Trust the process. Don't think about what the fear is, could be, or should be. Don't even to try to understand why you are painting your fear. Hold the intention in your heart to be shown a fear that you want to release via color, shape, and form. Remember, you don't need the story; you just need to follow the energy, the movement, the call and response from your heart to your gut to your hand. Notice what you are feeling, how you feel, and keep on moving.

Set up your space. Take a deep breath in, and ground yourself. Welcome in the Elements and your guides. Ask for a founda-tion blessing.

- Stand in front of your paper. Close your eyes and take some deep balancing breaths.

- Ask your heart to bring forth the fear that is blocking you at this moment. Notice all of your body sensations.

- Now ask the fear what is the first color, shape, or form that wants to come forth.

- Start to paint. Keep following your fear's lead.

- Keep breathing, and follow the energy.

- Ignore the story if one shows up.

- *As you paint your fear, it shines a little light on it and makes it a little less scary.*

A STORY
Blindsided

A few years back, my intuitive self called me to paint big, with lots of paint on paper. (I loved the way those paintings made me feel!) I was painting at a week-long retreat, which allowed for a slower and deeper unfolding of what my intuitive self wanted to show me. I didn't try to *make* a feeling come up or create a story around feelings that arose. I just kept painting. While I was painting, the priority was to listen deeply to my inner self, to have a call and response from my heart — to paint — to paper. Little by little, one tiny revelation, would show up. I would mutter, "Oh ... really ... wow," then keep on painting.

I took the paper off the wall and moved it onto the ground. I felt compelled to start walking, actually pacing in circles on the paper. Paint squished between my toes. I kept walking, having no idea what was bubbling up. I was only aware of the pull to keep walking. I fully trusted in the process, the divine guidance of my heart, my creative soul, my intuitive muse, and kept on walking. Once in awhile, I would throw red paint at the center or stab at the center, but I didn't know why. I was truly following the energy. I must have walked miles over the next few days. During the last half hour of the retreat, I looked over with laser focus at a very simple drawing of the four directions that I had done earlier that day. In the center, I had written YOU. I picked up the drawing and threw it into the center of the painting, where I was pacing around. That simple act, after painting and pacing for almost five days, brought forth the clarity that I was painting/pacing forth self-hatred. In a million years, I would have never thought that I harbored self-hatred. But there it was, clear as day in the middle of my footprints. I looked at it, felt the truth of it, recognized behaviors that perpetuated that belief in me. I shook. I cried. I then bowed to the painting and the creative guidance inside me. Now my dirty little secret was out in the open, in the light, for me to consider, explore, heal, and keep on painting.

I would have never gone to this place directly. It was the guidance of my intuitive creative self, safely searching, requiring me to bring my shadow parts out into the open. And that big secret showed up in a way I could manage, look at, and process. This manifested as ending friendships that no longer served me and changing my work so that it still was deep and meaningful but allowed for more self-expression and more travel.

We all have these dark, scary, don't-want-to-admit-to-the-world feelings. But when those feelings get in the way of our being whole and authentic in the world, it is time to bring them to the light, let them go, and let healing happen.

Perfectionism overrated: be perfectly you

Why is this in the Be Brave section, you may ask? Well, my friends, your inner perfectionist can get in the way of you being fully you, just as much as fear or self-hatred. Doing the right thing. Being the right thing. Being what everyone else expects of you. This is all part of your inner perfectionist, and it's exhausting!

There are different ways the critic shows up. The saboteur, that does exactly what it sounds like, sabotages all your good ideas, thoughts, and dreams. The critic tells you everything you do is *wrong*. The more subtle inner perfectionist says, "If you can't do it right, don't do it at all."

In the creative world, your inner perfectionist shows up as:

- Painting the right way, drawing straight lines, or staying in the lines
- Making things look like they should
- Being neat and tidy, looking perfect

Adult learners always feel that they should be experts at whatever they are learning immediately. Did that reinforcement start with coloring books? Maybe. We can be very hard on ourselves, judgmental and easily frustrated, especially when we can't get it right the first time.

Lets face it: Perfectionism can be one of your biggest demons. Perfectionism keeps you from being at ease, exploring for the sake of exploring, being open to the unexpected, showing up, and having fun.

CREATE

INNER PERFECTIONIST PAINT PARTY

Let's try an experiment. Set up your sacred painting space. Get grounded and centered. Ask your inner Perfectionist to come out and play. Revel in her/him. Let her/him be all that s/he is — all uptight, neat crisp, Miss/Mr. Know-it-all, Miss/Mr. I-got-this, Miss/Mr. All-neat-and-tidy.

Get prepared:

- Now, go ahead — measure, grab a ruler.

- Make sure the colors match the way they should. Have fun inviting this part of you to play. And if you get stuck, get more exacting.

- Notice how your body feels as it paints from your inner perfectionist. How do you feel in your heart? What is happening in your thoughts?

- Take a moment to do a body scan. Notice the tight spots, the open spaces, notice everything, and record it in your mental notebook under perfectionism. That way you'll know when your inner perfectionist shows up, even uninvited. You will be able to choose whether to invite that part of you to play or whether to override your inner perfectionist in that moment.

Body feeling helps you know what is in your way, whether it's your inner perfectionist or deep sadness. The more you understand what creates these patterns in you, the more control you have over your life. Go ahead — get exacting.

Heal thy Heart

In Asian medicine, the heart is our sovereign energy and life force. The Heart (spirit), mind/emotions, and physical body are all entwined into one. The Heart is considered to be the vessel that all experiences and expressions move through. In health, the Heart holds onto nothing. From the perspective of Asian medicine, if your experiences, expressions, and emotions get stuck in your heart, it's a major cause of illness and can put your whole being in jeopardy.

Here is an example of how stuck emotions can translate into illness. If someone you love dies, and grief goes on too long, you become vulnerable. This disrupts the balance in your meridians, chakras, and auric fields. Your *bodymindspirit* then translates that imbalance into depression, anxiety, feeling lost or heartbroken, which can ultimately lead to a heart attack, asthma, and/or a limiting belief.

The heart is the sovereign of all organs & represents the consciousness of one's being. It is responsible for intelligence, wisdom & spiritual transformation.

—Yellow Emperor's Classic of Medicine

Above all else, guard your heart, for it is the wellspring of life.

— Proverbs 4:23

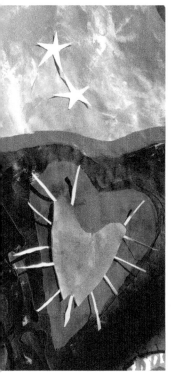

According to Oriental medicine, the seven emotions that can injure the heart are: fear, anger, fright, grief, joy, worry, pensiveness (overthinking).

If an event in your life created hurt, and that hurt stuck in your heart, the stuck emotion begins to block the energetic vitality of the heart. This slows the heart chakra's movement, then clogs up the heart meridian energy, which disrupts the function of the heart organ itself.

To shift, change, and heal your heartbreak, you need to clear that muscle memory pattern from your original heartbreak in the layers of your auric fields, chakras, meridians (body), limiting beliefs (mind), and your subconscious (spirit). You can do this by becoming consciously aware of your subconscious holding patterns. Your awareness restores balance and harmony to your system.

In Western medicine, we gain access to this original heartbreak in many different ways. Commonly, we can talk our heartbreak out with a counselor. Yet, sometimes that first original heartbreak is so deep inside, so preverbal, that your mind can't access it with words. This is where the powerful combination of preverbal access (intuitive painting) *plus* counseling can allow your heartbreak to heal.

To access our preverbal subconscious knowledge, we use our intuitive creative intelligence that speaks to us in the language of the subconscious—color, shape, and form. On one level, everything we do in this book is centered around healing your heart and original heartbreaks. Our original heart hurts have many layers over them; many stories to explain why we feel this way.

Your have learned the process, looked at your demons, and regained vitality. Now let's dive deeper to bring healing to your hurt. Starting to heal that original hurt will build vitality in your emotional heart and physical heart.

Intention, belief, trust, and acceptance are the tools to heal your heart. Intention is powerful. Ninety-five percent of what we do is intention the other 5% is tools, techniques, time, and money. So let's use our powerful intention as a catalyst for healing your heart.

What if ...

> *What if we ask for a creative expression to heal our heart fully?*

> *What if we trust our inner self to guide us to the place where love and healing can restore vitality to our hearts?*

Namaste. (I bow to your inner heart light from my inner heart light)

CREATE

TRANSFORMING HEARTBREAK

Yes, on some level this is what all the exercises in this book are getting at: Sharpen your intention and focus to see what shows up, to transform your heartbreak.

Remember you will only experience what you are ready for; much of this work happens in your subconscious layers.

For now, be open to shining some creative light on your original heart hurt.

Set up your space. Close your eyes. Take a deep breath in, and ground yourself. Welcome in the Elements and your guides. Ask for a foundation blessing and write those on your paper, or hold them in your heart.

- Be gentle and kind to yourself.

- Be open to exploring your original heartache.

- Invite your original heartache/hurt/break to come forth and be painted. Don't worry about naming your heart hurt; just explore it with your intuitive self in a dialogue of call and response.

- Keep breathing.

- Smile into your heart.

- Let your whole experience be led by your intuitive self, to your heart, to hand, to paint, to paper.

- As you unfurl and release the stuck emotions in your heart, your heart energy becomes clearer. The higher your heart energy vibration is, the brighter you will be in the world.

This is the first, wildest,
wisest thing I know:
The soul exists ... it
is built entirely out of
attentiveness.

— Mary Oliver

Be Bold — Resonance Creates Change

Understanding a limiting belief creates resonance that leads to change in your *bodymindspirit* muscle memory and acts as a catalyst for deep healing. Now that you have cleared out the old, stale, stuck, no-longer-hidden stuff, your focus shifts to reconfiguring your energy patterns. Think of it like this: You have taken the old silverware out of its drawer, and now you are beginning to shine it up and make it sparkle.

Healing occurs when you focus on a particular intention and then allow the intelligence of your intuitive creative self to share bits of learning — showing you your blind spots and new aspects of yourself to grow into.

This is the place where your spirit and body meet.

When you work at the subtle energy levels of the body (auric fields, meridians, chakras) you can change limiting beliefs or trapped emotions that are stuck in your energetic system. Then your newly rebalanced energy patterns filter down into the body level to create change, starting to shift toward your *true bodymindspirit's* cellular muscle memory.

Our process of change can be messy—it's not all unicorns, fairy tales, soft and fuzzy. You still look at your blind spots to experience new areas of yourself that can use growth.

Be bold.

Be radiant.

Be you.

Paint your chakras

Chakras are energy vortexes, centers or hubs of life force that move the energy throughout the body. Originating from Hindu spiritual traditions, chakra in Sanskrit means wheel. Since 1927, we have been familiar with seven main chakras from two translated texts: the *Sat-chakra-Nirupana*, and the *Padaka-Pancaka*, by Sir John Woodroffe. Our chakras reflect our lifelong situations.

Every thought and experience you've ever had in your life gets filtered through these chakra databases. Each event is recorded into your cells… in effect your biography becomes your biology.

— Caroline Myss, *Anatomy of the Spirit* (1996)

In this section we will explore each chakra separately, so we can attain a more intimate understanding of that particular energy in us. You will get to know what each chakra feels like energetically, understand where your chakra energy is stuck, where it needs to be cleared, where it's sluggish, and what each chakra has to teach you. Each

creative act will focus on one chakra. You will learn to clear, stimulate, balance, and heal that chakra, just by following the instructions from your creative muse. As always in your creative ventures, what shows up for you will not always match the written information about the chakras. No worries — just be open to what shows up.

When I facilitate the chakra painting series, I combine music, simple yoga poses, and an easy overview about that particular chakra. Sometimes I teach all seven over two and a half days; some classes are weekly, one chakra per week, or one chakra per month. The longer the time between classes, the more personal changes and learnings that bubble up to the surface for students.

Our *bodymind* holds cellular muscle memory, and our subtle body energies do too. Righting your energy field and *bodymind* systems takes time to maintain change. The more you clear out old patterns, the more your, original, true self-blueprint is brought forward, changing dense energy patterns to more enlivened vital life force.

Some suggestions while working on your chakra paintings exploration: Work on one chakra at a time. Start with chakra one, then two, etc. How long you spend on each chakra and how much time your take between each chakra is up to you. You can work on one painting the whole time, which will hold the energy of all seven chakras. You can make a "My journey through the chakras" book and paint each of your chakra journeys in a large journal. Feel for the rhythm that is right for you. Trust your intuition.

CREATE

RAINBOW HEALING

Set up your painting space. Create your sacred space. Ground yourself. Ask for a foundation blessing.

- For each chakra: set up your supplies.

- Play music for that chakra(s).

- Read over the short description for each chakra you have decided to explore.

- If it feels right for you, do the seed sound, chant, and yoga for the chakra you are working with (described below).

- Allow your intuitive creative muse to lead you with color, shape, and form to express your unique expression of each chakra. Allow energy to show up however it wishes; don't try to make it *fit* into what you know about the chakra. Enjoy getting to know your personal movement of each chakra.

You may use the following chakra guide* for your explorations. To help you on your journey, you'll find descriptions, affirmations, music and yoga poses that correspond with each chakra.

First chakra Muladhara (root)

Location:	Base of the spine, foundation of the heart
Element:	Earth
Color:	Red
Sense:	Smell
Purpose:	Grounding, survival, stability, self-sufficiency, connection into our bodies
Basic rights:	To be here and have what is needed to survive
Gifts:	Health, prosperity, security, group identity, and a dynamic presence
Organs:	Adrenal glands, organs of elimination (kidney, skin, colon), bones, hair, nails, legs
Affirmations:	I belong. I am here. I am enough. May I be able to nourish and nurture myself. May I be grounded, stable, and feel connected to the oneness of life/universe.
Seed sound:	LAM

Music to awaken this chakra:

· *Rhythms of the Chakras*, "Origins," Glen Velez
· *Chakra Beatbox*, "Elephant Power," MC Yogi
· *Back to the Earth*, "When I Woke," Rusted Root
· *Chakra Healing Chants*, "Gaia Shekinah Nama Om," Sophia

Yoga poses to activate this chakra: bridge, child, half warrior

*Adapted from *Wheels of Life* by Anodea Judith

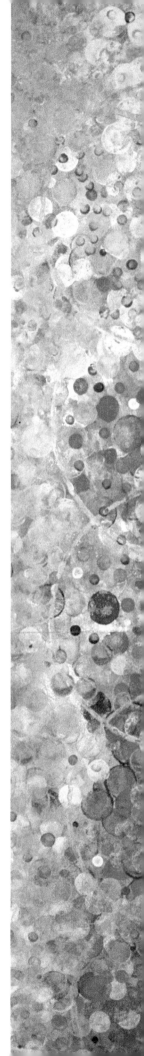

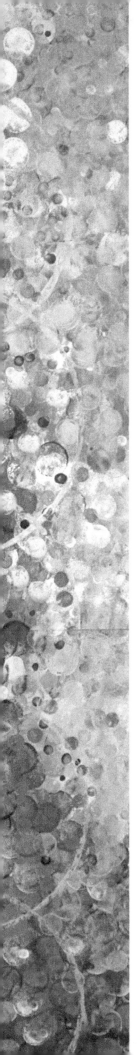

Second chakra: Svadhisthana (sweetness)

Location:	Sacrum
Element:	Water
Color:	Orange
Sense:	Senses
Purpose:	Movement, connection, creativity, sensuality
Basic rights:	To feel and have pleasure
Gifts:	Movement, from survival to pleasure (emotional, sexuality)
Organs:	Abdomen, lower back, sexual organs
Affirmations:	I embrace my feelings and my sexuality. Life is pleasurable. I move readily and effortlessly.
Seed Sound:	VAM

Music to awaken this chakra:

- *Chakra Healing Zone*, "Svadhisthana," Robin Silver
- *Chakra Healing Chants*, "Uma … Jai Ma!" Sophia
- *Rhythms of the Chakras*, "Fruits of Labor," Glen Velez

Yoga poses to activate this chakra: belly breathing, spinal flex, camel, and eagle

Third chakra Manipuri (lustrous gem)

Location:	Behind the solar plexus
Element:	Fire
Color:	Yellow
Sense:	Sight/psychic intuition
Purpose:	Ego, self-definition, will power
Basic rights:	To act and be an individual, to be free
Gifts:	Ego, intuition, self-esteem, activity, individuation, will, proactivity, power
Organs:	Eyes, liver, gallbladder, digestive tract, stomach, the endocrine system
Affirmations:	I honor the power within me. I accomplish tasks easily and effortlessly. The fire within me burns through all blocks and fears. I can do whatever I will to do.
Seed Sound:	RAM

Music to awaken this chakra:

- *Healing Chants*, "The Orbit / Nam Myoho," Sophia
- *Rhythms Of The Chakras*, "Mirrors," Glen Velez
- *Chakra Healing Zone*, "3rd Chakra — Manipura," Win Meyerson

Yoga poses to activate this chakra: archer, boat, sun meditation

Fourth chakra Anahata (the sound of one hand clapping)

Location:	Heart
Element:	Air
Color:	Emerald green
Sense:	Touch
Purpose:	Love and balance
Basic rights:	To love and be loved
Gifts:	Love, balance, self-love, kindheartedness, devotion, relationship, intimacy, reaching out, taking in
Organs:	Heart, lungs
Affirmations:	I am worthy of love. I am loving to myself and others. There is an infinite supply of love. I live in balance with others.
Seed Sound:	YAM

Music to awaken this chakra:

- *Chakra Healing Zone*, "4th Chakra – Anahata," David & Steve Gordon
- *Waking the Cobra*, "Golden Wind, Emerald Star (Yahm)," Vocal Medicine Baird Hersey
- *Heart Chakra Meditation*, "The Inner Temple," Karunesh
- *Chakra Healing Chants*, "Heart of Earth," Sophia

Yoga poses to activate this chakra: Alternative nose breathing. Hands stretched back to open your chest. Thymus tap (your thymus is located in the middle of your breast bone)

Fifth chakra Vishudda (purification)

Location:	Throat
Element:	Ether
Color:	Bright blue
Sense:	Sound and resonance
Purpose:	Communication and creative expression
Basic rights:	To speak and hear truth
Gifts:	Communication, creativity, listening, resonance, finding one's own voice, self-expression, creative identity
Organs:	Throat, thyroid, voice
Affirmations:	I speak and hear the truth. I express myself with clear intent. Creativity flows in and through me. My voice is necessary.
Seed Sound:	HAM

Music to awaken this chakra:

- *Chakra Healing Chants*, "Thy Song (Fifth chakra)," Sophia
- *Chakra Healing Zone*, "5th Chakra –Vishudda," David & Steve Gordon
- *Rhythms of the Chakras*, "Voices," Glen Velez

Yoga poses to activate this chakra: chin press breath, neck rolls/shrugs, fish

Sixth chakra Ajna (third eye)

Location:	Brow, third eye
Element:	Light
Color:	Indigo
Sense:	Sight
Purpose:	Pattern recognition, knowing transcendent realms, vision
Basic rights:	To see
Gifts:	Clairvoyance, telepathy, wisdom, connection to higher self, imagination, dreams, ideas, transforming the individual "I" into something transpersonal
Organs:	Eyes, pineal gland
Affirmations:	I see all things in clarity. I am open to the wisdom within. I can manifest my vision.
Seed Sound:	AUM

Music to awaken this chakra:

- *Chakra Healing Zone*, "6th Chakra — Ajna," Sophia
- *Chakra Healing Chants*, "Infinite Wisdom (Sixth chakra)," Sophia
- *Rhythms of the Chakras*, "Third-eye," Glen Velez

Yoga poses to activate this chakra: humming bee breath, cat/cow, OM meditation (namaste at 3rd eye)

Seventh chakra Sahasrara (union)

Location:	Cerebral cortex
Element:	Earth
Color:	Violet
Sense:	Truth and divinity within
Purpose:	Understanding, expansion
Basic Rights:	To know and to learn
Gifts:	Liberation, self-knowledge, wisdom, transcendence, immanence, belief systems, higher power, divinity, union, vision
Organs:	Top of your head, brain, fontanel
Affirmations:	Divinity resides within. I am open to new ideas. Information I need comes to me. The world is my teacher. I am guided by higher power. I am guided by inner wisdom.
Seed Sound:	NG (AUM)

Music to awaken this chakra:

- *Chakra Healing Zone*, "7th Chakra," Shajan
- *Chakra Healing Chants*, "Be Still (Seventh chakra)," Sophia
- *Chakra Healing Zone*, "Transcendence - Kundalini Rising," Karmacosmic
- *Heart Chakra Meditation*, "The Inner Temple," Karunesh

Yoga poses to activate this chakra: breath of balance "I am balanced between heaven and earth." Thunderbolt/Rock, "I am at peace with myself."

Auric fields: many layers of you

Our aura refers to the layers of energy fields that surround our physical body; like energetic halos surrounding our whole bodies — feeling, filtering, infusing, and imbuing us with energy from our environment. The auric fields move into our body and create our chakras. This is the world of *bodymind*. This body knows the past, present, and future.

It's a protective energy; sometimes it's an intermediary between our environment and our physical body. Quantum physics tells us that energy and matter are interchangeable, and looking at the auric energy you can see that is true.

Traditional spiritual paintings have been showing us these auric energy fields for millenniums. Halos, the gold light around their top of their heads, are always shown around enlightened beings, reminding us that they are higher vibration beings.

Notice how the colors of the auric fields are the same as the chakra color associations and the color progression of a rainbow.

LAYER 1

Etheric Body, 1/4–1 inch away from your physical body

This is the closest layer to your physical body. It is where your meridian template resides, and it represents your health. It holds a similar vibration to the first chakra.

LAYER 2

Emotional Body, around 3 inches away from your physical body

This layer holds the vibration of your inner feelings. Sometimes called *the etheric double*, it mimics the physical shape of your body and holds a similar vibration to the second chakra.

LAYER 3

Mental body, 3–8 inches away from your physical body

This is the layer of the mind, your thoughts and related to your ego/will. You feel emotions at this level. It holds a similar vibration to the third (solar plexus) chakra. *This is your true life force and the only aura layer that radiates and absorbs energy from the environment.* The other layers in the aura only absorb energy. This layer holds a similar vibration to the third chakra.

LAYER 4

Astral body, 6–12 inches away from your physical body

This layer is related to the heart chakra (4th). It is a bridge between denser (physical) and higher vibrations (spiritual). This is your soul plane. It allows for full the expression of your body, your mind, your spirit. This layer also holds all your past and present life stories.

LAYER 5

Etheric template, 18–24 inches away from your physical body

This is the layer where energy work healing happens, including in the creative intuitive realm. Here you process, clear out, shift, and balance. This layer holds the etheric blueprint of your physical body. When change occurs here, it filters down and changes your physical body as well. This layer also holds a similar vibration to your throat chakra.

LAYER 6

Celestial body, 24–30 inches away from your physical body

Your higher self resides here. It's your intuitive level, your higher mind function. It's your intellectual link with the Creator and encourages your processes of enlightenment. This layer also holds a similar vibration to your third eye chakra.

LAYER 7

Causal body, 24–40 inches away from your physical body

This layer contains our soul's contract — it holds all the experiences your soul has encountered. It is related to the seventh (crown) chakra, which is your divine, or universal consciousness.

CREATE

MANY LAYERS OF YOU

Let's explore your auric layers. See what energy shows up as your explore, refine, and bring balance to your auric layers, which are the colors of the rainbow

Set up your painting space. Create your sacred space. Ground yourself. Ask for a foundation blessing.

- Close your eyes, and bring your awareness to the air on your skin. Extend your awareness out further, and feel the vibrations of your auric fields.

- Don't worry about defining the individual layers, stay connected with the auric fields' vibration around your as you paint. Let that vibration inform color, shape, and form.

- Feel vibration ... paint vibration.

Remember, you have directed your intuitive creative self to explore your auric fields. What you need to experience will appear. Just follow the brush and the energy, and see what comes forth.

The beauty of this intuitive creative work is, everything that shows up during the creative process will inform you about the state of your auric layers, then the process will clear, shift, and rebalance them.

Be Open ... GLOW!

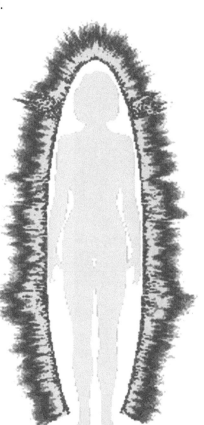

Gas discharge visualization (GDV) electrophonic imaging of the human bio-field

Return of the body parts

Every part of our *bodymindspirit* has energy and vitality. Long-term trauma to a body part will reduce life force in that particular body part, creating illness.

There is a shamanic healing technique that calls back the life force of a traumatized body part, restoring healthy energy. (We know that healing happens when you bring back life force, so why not to a body part?)

In this exercise, adapted from shamanic healing concepts, you will paint a healing talisman for one of your body parts. As you paint, you will infuse healing energy with every brushstroke, which will call your body part's life force energy back. Your focus can be on a physical pain, an emotional sensation, or you can allow this creative talisman to represent a limiting belief. If none of those things shows up, you can do one of two things: Make a cup of tea and put your feet up. Or close your eyes, and sense if a part of your body is trying to get your attention — feel for tingling, niggling sensations, a memory that pops into your mind, or a feeling that suddenly shows up. That will be your starting place. Ask your intuitive self to heal whatever part of you needs to be healed.

CREATE

BODY PART HEALING

Set up your painting space. Create your sacred space.
Ground yourself. Ask for a foundation blessing.

- Bring all your awareness to the body part you
  want to balance.

- Notice how the area around that body part
  feels. Is it heavy, so light that it feels invisible or
  missing? (whether that physical part is still there
  or not).

- What does the vibration feel like? Is it bright, dull,
  pulsing, piercing?

- Tell that body part that you would like to paint a
  healing for it, to return its life force.

- Let that life force energy communicate with you
  in color, shape, and form. Be open to whatever
  energy shows up, and how it shows up and start
  there.

Part of the healing nature of this creative process is to
bring back life force. So go ahead and talk to your body.
Make a creative talisman for a part of yourself that
wants to be infused with life force again.

> **Milagros (Spanish for miracle) are small**
> **charms empowered with healing prayers**
> **for a particular body part.**

Getting to know all sides of you

Knowing your feminine and masculine energies is essential to a healthy life. Whether you are male or female, you have both masculine energy and feminine energy in you. I like to think of them as *balancing* each other, rather than opposing forces or opposites.

FEMININE	MASCULINE
Moon	Sun
Earth	Heaven
Dark	Light
Death	Life

Keeping and balancing your feminine and masculine energies is the basis of most major healing modalities. To be in balance with both energies, polar aspects of ourselves, will allow us to be whole and maintain our health.

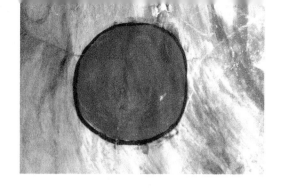

HOT	COLD
Hard	Yielding
Masculine	Feminine

There are some cultural biases against being strong in both masculine and feminine aspects. When you shift out of defined feminine or masculine categories, society freaks out and feels threatened — then labels appear. For example, *real men don't wear pink*. False. Men who are comfortable with their feminine and masculine aspects can, in fact, wear pink. Think of the Scots, fierce warriors in kilts (skirts). Or the powerful Hawaiian Kahunas — adorned in flowers and wearing sarongs (skirts). They have no problem showing both the feminine and masculine parts of themselves.

We are more fluid in our expessions of our feminine and masculine energies than what we see represented in our culture. For example, a man can express his feelings and cry—he doesn't need to be the strong and silent type. A woman can support her family and allow her husband to be a stay-at-home parent. It is vitally important to reclaim both sides *regardless* of what sex you are.

Labels wound. When we paint, we acknowledge hurtful labels and allow those self-limiting labels to **drop away.**

CREATE

BALANCE

Your inner muse is closely connected to your feminine and masculine energy. The creative process will show you both aspects of yourself and where those energies meet, expand, then balance.

Set up your painting space. Create your sacred space. Ground yourself. Ask for a foundation blessing.

- Ask your intuitive self which energy it wants to explore first, masculine or feminine.

- As your feminine and masculine parts coalesce into color, shape, and form, let your masculine and feminine vibration emerge however the energy moves you. Let the shapes be what they want to be. In other words, everything can be topsy-turvy — ups are downs — downs are sideways.

Allow you intuitive self to lead the way.

Your *bodymindspirit* will start to vibrate in that masculine/feminine energy, balancing, enlivening, and making both energies more accessible to you.

Try exploring just one side at a time. After you have done separate masculine and feminine energy paintings, invite those energies to unite, interweave, and integrate onto one creation.

Two sides make a balanced *you*.

Where your spirit and body meet

The meaning of spirit is personal and held differently in our hearts. The heart energy that gives us life, movement, inspiration, and a greater sense of ourselves; is one of the many expressions of spirit.

We have looked at the energetic systems of our bodies in order to understand the many layers of ourselves, and move deeper into the sublime, navigable energy where *spirit and body meet*.

Sublime: grand, awe inspiring, outstanding, a supreme gift from the Divine.

CREATE

SUBLIME MEETING

Let in your intuitive self, who speaks through the creative act of deep communion with color, shape, and form.

Experience the place where your *body and spirit meet.* As you paint, let sublime vibration of your Divine energy fill you.

Once you bring this sublime vibrational meeting place into form using paint on paper, your body and mind will have a muscle memory access point, so each time you go back to this place, your true self *remembers and expands.*

Set up your painting space. Create your sacred space. Ground yourself. Ask for a foundation blessing.

- Connect with your breath and your heart.

- Allow your breath to touch that sublime place where your *spirit and body meet.*

- Let your breath expand even more, fully allowing the vibration where your *spirit and body meet* to resonate through you and light up every cell in you and your subtle energies around you.

- Ask your wise, intuitive muse to express that energy into a form with color, and shape.

Meet ... paint ... expand. Light up!

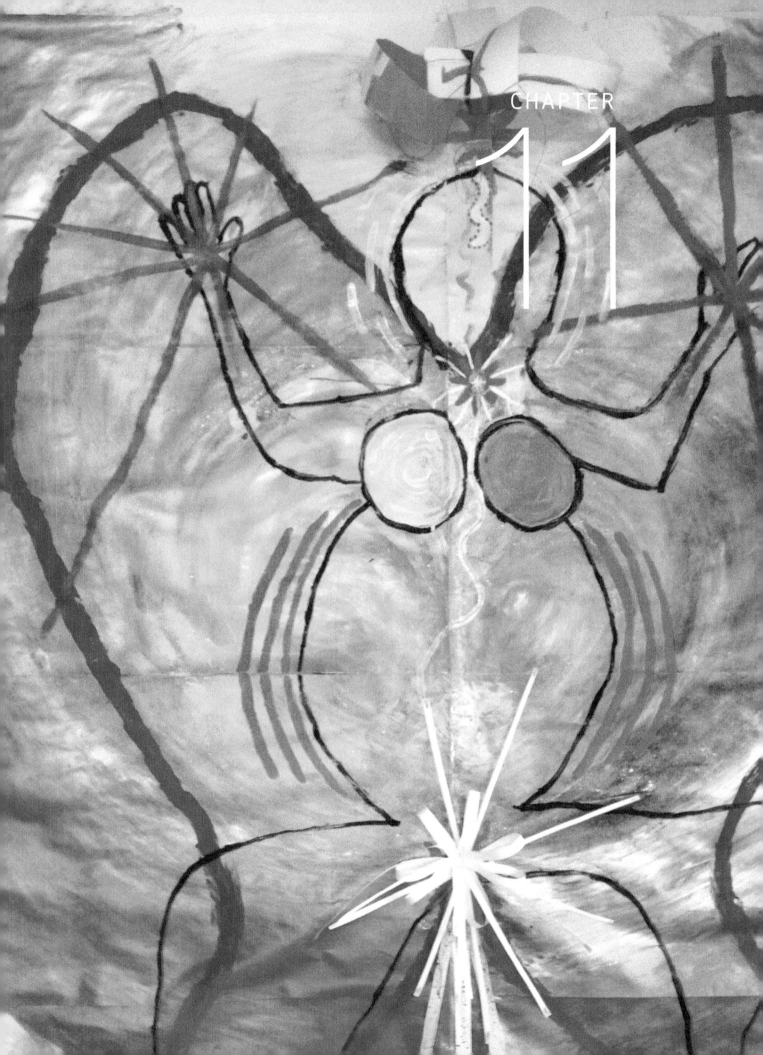

Go Beyond – Your Power Pieces

Traditionally totem poles come from the indigenous people of the Pacific Northwest. Their totem poles are often carved with various animals or people, which depict a story or a message to the community. Figures are stacked from bottom to top, often, with the most important figure on the top. Looking at t*he low man on the totem pole*, we usually understand that the bottom figure is small and compressed, a less important figure. However, totem poles are not always that literal or linear.

Typically, the more earthly energies are represented at the bottom of the totem poles. Higher on the totem pole, closer to the sky, we find heavenly energy. Contemporary, nontraditional totem poles are often created to represent a personal power object (talisman) for the individual. Often, a figure represents an individual, with seven images or shapes that loosely correspond to each chakra, or images that represent personal guardian spirits. These totems often represent the individual's energy/power.

Create your personal totem

A totem painting is a representation of the healing energy that now empowers you: your guardian angel, power animal, God energy, and superhero. In this exploration, I invite you to create your own totem. This will be the first painting that represents the *new you* and becomes a talisman, a power-filled piece of art. Now that you have spent time exploring and clearing old beliefs, shifting dense energy patterns, you are going to bring your power-filled self out into the world in the form of a painting representing the clearer, stronger, more harmonious you.

When you create, at least two things happen:

1. Energetic manifestation: When you paint, you bring your energy, your true power, into the world. This positive shift in our energy creates a blueprint for positive changes in our physical bodies too.

2. Physical manifestion: When you paint, you bring all the new learning from your *bodymindspirit* energy fields into physical form (the painting). Through the act of creating, moving your body, and engaging your mind, that new energy starts to change your being.

Let me introduce you to a different way to access your intuitive creative self, using a variation on the shamanic journey method. Here is a simple way to explore a shamanic journey.

Recall that shamanism is in communion with everything around us — everything around us is alive and has spirit. Time and space have no boundaries. We have helping spirits that have a higher perspective on our human, embodied life.

The shamanic journey is one small part of shamanism. It allows you to connect and learn from The Spirit That Lives In All Things. By connecting with your higher self, or your guardian energy, you connect with an energy that has a higher perspective than you do on the earthly plane. The shamanic journey is a way to step out of your mind, to spark a dialogue with your guardian spirits much like a conversation with your intuitive self.

Learning about your totem energies or guardian powers will help you understand your unique *gifts* and the power that lives deep inside your bones. The shamanic journey will help you focus your *intention* to meet your totem energy and create a physical manifestation of that energy via the creative process. All you need is an open heart, trust, and a desire to learn about yourself. Use all of your senses as you move into the journey, and then give the journey over to your helping spirits, and let the information that best serves you at this moment in time to come forth.

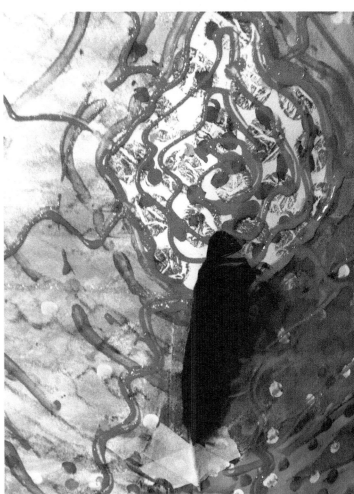

CREATE

SHAMANIC MEETING

A steady precussive beat will help you shift into non-ordinary space.* *Set up your painting space. Create your sacred space. Ground yourself. Ask for a foundation blessing.*

- Imagine yourself in nature, somewhere that's familiar and comforting for you.

- Feel the earth under your feet. Feel the temperature of the air against your skin.

- What do you see? What do you sense?

- Keep repeating to yourself: I want to meet my helping spirit to be shown what my power totems look like — via color, shape, and form.

- Imagine a ball of red yarn with one end tied around your heart. Throw it forward as you ask to meet your helping spirit and see your power totems in color, shape, and form.

- The ball will land just where you need to be. Notice the landscape. What do you see, hear, feel, sense? Is there an energy presence?

- Thank your healing spirit for being there and tell it that you would like to create a totem painting that represents your personal power. Ask it, "Please show

*go to DaminiCelebre.com

me what my totem would look and feel like." Take in all that you experience. Know that your creative muse will translate that vibrational information into color, shape, and form.

- You can ask for specific information with each part or layer of your totem pole (all at once or one part at a time). Or you can start painting with the help of your helping spirit and see what shows up.

- How do you feel as you bring your personal power vibration forward with paint on paper?

A shamanic journey is not always a technicolor film. The more you use your senses, the more information you will receive.

You can use a multistep process. You may want to take several short journeys: painting after each journey, building on one painting.

Or you may choose to ask for all your information at once, take some notes, and then start painting. Let your intuitive self and helping spriits guide you along the way. Remember you can always journey again to gather information.

The only rules you need to follow are your own. Just be open to the vibration and energetic force of your totem energy. Paint first—interpret later (if you must).

Allow yourself to fill up with the goodness of your power.

Your inner god and goddess

Mythology is found throughout many ancient cultures: Greek, Roman, Indian, Sumerian, Asian. Myths are stories that bring complex information to life. In mythology, gods and goddesses are the all-powerful parental figures that often were held out as role models. The myriad god/goddess personalities are various reflections of us. Stories tell us of how power is used, misused, and what the lessons are. They show us different aspects of ourselves, whether hidden or realized — the warrior, oracle, healer, mother, father, and mischievous imp. Often though, gods and goddesses are not accessible to us on this earthly plane.

I propose a different way of thinking about mythology: looking through the lens of our individual mythology. Let's assume that all-powerful god/goddess energy is already within us; it just needs to be awakened. Imagine the possibility that we are a reflection of all the energies out there — like many facets of a diamond, or in this case, the Divine One, the Light, our archetype of the god/goddess.

A myth is a sacred narrative explaining how the world and humankind assumed their present form.

— Alan Dundes

Have you experienced the energy of divine oneness for a brief moment? The mystics of India refer to it as a *satori*, which is a Japanese Buddhist word for awakening or enlightenment. We all have a god/ goddess part in us, and your intuitive creative self wants to share it with you via color, shape, and form.

Through the creative process, call forth that god/goddess energy that lives inside every cell, and, using your creative muse, allow that energy to move from your unconscious and integrate into your consciousness. Call forward that energy, bring it into your energy fields, chakras, meridians, DNA, RNA, *bodymindspirit* muscle movement, so that as you create, you reawaken your god/goddess inside you.

CREATE

THE GOD'S SPARK IN YOU

Set up your painting space. Create your sacred space. Ground yourself. Ask for a foundation blessing.

- *Recall your perfect divine energy.* Bring it to your conscious awareness and consciously invite that god/goddess-like energy inside you to come forth and be expressed through your heart and body.

- Move it, dance it, sing it, and paint it. Experience that god/goddess-like energy moving through you. Let your body move as you create. Move your body in new ways, releasing old stagnant ways of being.

- Connect with your deep cell memory where your divine spark lives. That energy can be hard to describe. That's why we use the language of our unconscious (color, shape, and form) to activate deep cell memory (the information of your inner god/goddess). In this way it can come forth a little at a time.

- With one brushstroke at a time, paint the inner aspect of who you are: goddess, god, saint, mystic, avatar.

- Put paint on paper, create a physical manifestation of your god/goddess vibration.

Your cellular muscle memory remembers this God's spark energy. Let it move up to your consciousness. This energy may appear in different ways. Let your all-knowing intuitive self bring forth what you need to know, feel, and move at the moment.

Don't hold back.

Your heart's call

Do you have a feeling that you are here at this time, on this planet, for a reason? Perhaps it feels like a half-remembered dream, a feeling, a vision, or a stirring in your heart. You *are here* for a purpose. You do have a *gift to bring forth.* Does this statement awaken something deep inside you? Does it make your eyebrows rise? Your eyes twinkle? Are you curious, excited, ready to bring that dream forth?

You have explored different way to know your true self with the creative process. Each time you create, you allow another aspect of yourself to come forward, recalling, reclaiming those longings, dreams, desires that you put away for safekeeping until the time is right. Well, the time is now. Time to *remember* the gift you have come into the world with — *it's time* to share it with yourself and the world.

I'm beautiful in my way 'cause god makes no mistakes. I'm on the right track, baby. I was born this way.

— Lady Gaga

CREATE

HEART'S CALL

Set up your painting space. Create your sacred space. Ground yourself. Ask for a foundation blessing.

- Take a deep breath in.

- Feel the place where your body meets the earth.

- Feel the energy come in from the Earth up through your feet to your heart, and down from the heavens to your head and into your heart.

- Feel that deep energy of purpose stirring in your heart.

- Ask your intuitive creative self to bring forth the vibration of your heart's call with color, shape, and form.

Your gifts will show up in many different ways. Leave your critic and your saboteur at the door. Don't judge or put a story to what shows up. Don't even try to make sense of it now. Just let your creative energy flow and your whole body remember.

You can do this exploration as a five-minute daily exercise in your journal, or as a daily exploration on one piece of paper. Layer over layer over weeks, months, or maybe years.

You may or may not have a clear picture of your heart's call, but as you paint it, you bring that vibration into form. Your mind may not understand it, but the many parts of you are ready to shine.

Paint your heart's gifts. Paint your beauty into the world. It will make the world a more beautiful place.

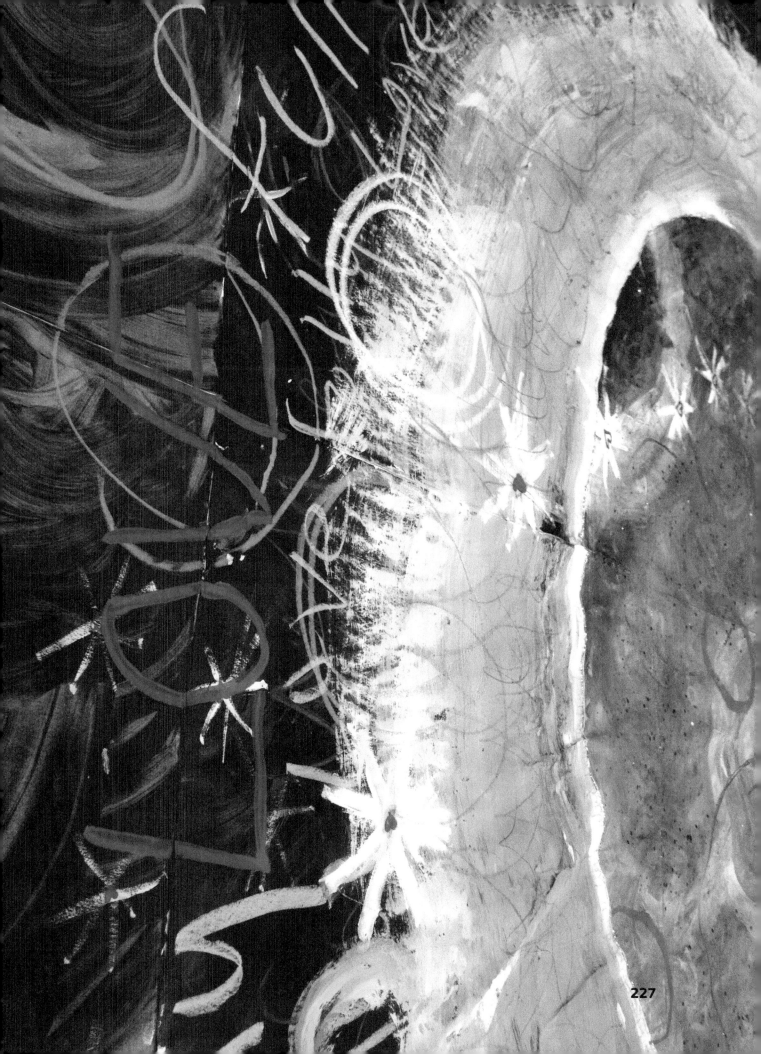

227

Paint your heart out

You have been healing, balancing, and welcoming back the many layers of your *bodymindspirit* as you have explored yourself through this book. You have shifted the dense and almost forgotten parts of yourself and brought back your light. You are now a different person than when you started. Really! Breathe that knowledge in. Honor your courage and hard work.

All the changes within you, including your actions and responses, have shifted (mind). Your energy fields, chakras, and muscle memory are more in alignment (body). And you are getting closer and closer to your authentic self (soul/spirit). You have changed how you feel about yourself and how you hold yourself in the world. Now it's time to go inward and have a *heart-to-heart conversation* with yourself, bring forth the heart of the one you are *becoming*.

Bring the change you've cultivated out into the world.

Acknowledge the *new you.*

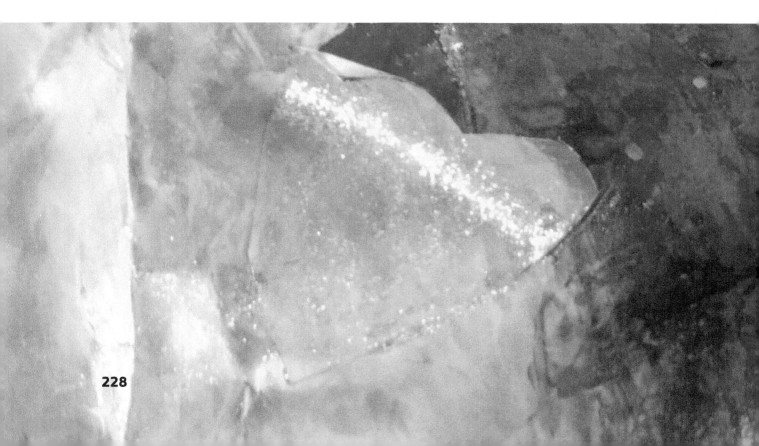

CREATE

PAINT YOUR HEART OUT

Set up your creative space with the intention of having a heart-to-heart with yourself.

Create your sacred space. Ground yourself.
Ask for a foundation blessing.

- Ask your wise all-knowing intuitive muse to show you a representation of your new heart vibration—via color, shape, and form. As always, don't guide it or direct it, just let your heart light flow.

- Notice how you feel as you paint your authentic heart.

- Let your heart vibration fill you and move your body, hands, paint, and brush.

You have worked hard and have created lots of changes. Now it is time to honor the authentic heart of you.

The New You!

What has shifted inside *you*? What feels different, more alive, and more awake?

Take some time and reflect on what *you* have learned about yourself. Reflect on the new parts of *you* that have emerged. The parts of *you* that were hidden in the shadows are now in full view. Those fragmented parts have returned home, whole, into *you*. Think of your subtle energy systems: your chakras, your meridians, your auric layers. Consider the otherworldly parts of yourself: your helping spirits, guardian angels, superheros. Reflect on new ways you think and respond in your body and mind. Think about the Divine energy swirling inside you.

CREATE

RADIANT YOU

Set up your painting space. Create your sacred space. Ground yourself. Ask for a foundation blessing.

- Take all of your newly accessed energy. Let these new vibrations circulate throughout your body, your mind, and your spirit. Let that energy fill you up, enlivening every cell.

- Call in your creative self to help you bring into form your whole-true-you vibration with paint to paper. Healing happens by shifting your subtle energies first, then rerouting those old patterns in your mind, and finally manifesting the changes in your body.

- As you paint your vibration, the body movement as you paint causes your *bodymindspirit* muscle memory to change, brings the new you into form (As above, so below; As within, so without).

- Take your time, savor all the movements. Let your body, your mind, and your spirit pulse, expand, and shimmer as you paint a creative representation of the *new you*.

Ritual and ceremony bring the magical into form, transform the ordinary into the sacred, bring the formless into form.

Initiation and Transition

Ceremony celebrates a transition, a big life event, a change in your life. A ceremony is a series of rituals combined. Focused by an intention to let go of unneeded parts in your life and to manifest change. This ceremony will help you solidify, bring into form, all the shifts you have experienced throughout the book: changes in your subtle energy fields, your muscle memory responses, even how you think differently. Ceremony announces to the world, energetically, *who you are*. Think of it as a *coming out party* for the *New You*.

Ceremony and ritual enact change. Rituals are daily actions that can maintain or instill new beliefs. Ritual can change your brain neural pathways. You do ritual daily, often unconsciously — kissing your kids goodbye, greeting the sun, gathering with family for a meal, blessing your food. These are all rituals.

Ceremony is a celebration that marks a seasonal highpoint, holiday, anniversary, or birthday, and in this case, a milestone, the *New You*. Both ceremony and ritual have a beginning, a middle, and an end.

This chapter is divided into three sections that build on one another. Together they create a ceremony to celebrate you. This ceremony will honor and celebrate all the new you.

One: Intention

When you bring your heart and your mind together, that is *intention*. Intention helps you clearly focus on what you desire to bring forth into the world.

To put this in chakra terms: your idea is a seed (1st chakra), it starts to grow (2nd chakra), and then you move it out into the world by your will (3rd chakra). This change goes to your heart (4th chakra), which is the pivot between Heaven and Earth.

Let the following exercise help you develop a clear intention of how you want to announce your New Self to the world.

ENERGY EXERCISE

Clear intention

- Spend some time getting quiet.

- Light a candle.

- Take a deep breath

- Feel the place where your body meets the earth. Feel the energy moving in your sublte energy fields.

- Welcome your guardian energies around you.

- Acknowledge the Elemental energies for giving you form.

- Ask your wise all-knowing creative self, how can you best to create an intention to share the New True You with the world. This can be with words, images, sound, dance.

- Keep exploring this until your intention is crystal clear.

Two: Letting go

Letting go can be powerful.

Letting go takes reflection, intention, deep listening and courage; all are vital parts of a ceremony. Letting go allows space for any last idea, issue, or concept that might be in your way. That last piece that you might need to let go, that last piece that keeps you from knowing the full truth of who you are. It's like removing the wrapping from a beautiful gift, and the gift is you. Release the last residual parts of yourself that protected you, but kept you from fully being alive.

You can release and let go with paint, sound, song, collage, dance; some or all of these techniques will work. Continue to let your intuitive self run the show, guide you, and bring forth what needs to be released, whether it's a story, a limiting belief, an event ... you name it.

CREATE

LET GO

Set up your painting space. Create your sacred space. Ground yourself. Ask for a foundation blessing.

- Take a deep breath and spend some time getting quiet.

- Feel the place where your body meets the Earth. Feel the energy coming into your body from the Earth and down from the heavens.

- Take a moment to express gratitude for your life and for this time that you have given yourself to know yourself better.

- Then from a place of deep gratitude, ask for the one idea that you need to let go of at this moment. Work with the first impression that comes to you.

- Once you have a sense of what you will be letting go of, ask for a color, shape, word, or dance that energetically represents what you are releasing.

- Don't limit your experience by trying to create an image of how your rational mind thinks it should look.

Go ahead—call forth your guardian energy, your inner muse and bring forth that last piece of information (for now) that will free you. Let the vibration of that move throughout your energetic fields and out into your physical realms. Allow your all-knowing intuitive muse, who has been leading you on the path of self-discovery show you what you need to let go.

Three: Manifesting

Ceremony can be done in any way that *feels* right for you.

Start by doing something that signifies the start of your ceremony, and create sacred space. You can light a candle, drum, dance, sing, pray, light incense, whatever action is meaningful to you. This is *your* celebration.

Take a few minutes and reflect on what has changed. What have you discovered about yourself since you started your journey? Notice how you feel when you account those changes in your body, mind, and spirit. Breathe in all your learnings, all the parts that you have welcomed home, your reclaimed powers, and all the gifts you recognize as yours. Take all of that change and beauty into your being with a breath, a smile, a bow to yourself and your inner muse.

You might want to make a little image, write a sentence, sing a song, or create a poem—some symbol that represents all of this change in you. Take a moment and consider if anything else wants to come forth—any desire, wish, dream, longing, and/or a prayer. After all, this is *your* manifestion ceremony.

ENERGY EXERCISE
Manifestation ceremony

- Create this ceremony in any way that resonates with you, focusing on how you want the *new you* to be perceived. Tell the world all about you. How would you name yourself? Would you keep your name or change it? What roles and responsibilities would you take on? Or let go of?

- Speak out loudly as the *new you*. Dance your dreams, play your symphony, and bring forth the *new you* to the universe.

- Feel your new vibration move out from your deep knowing place throughout your energy fields.

- Feel the resonance of your truth throughout your *bodymindspirit*.

- Let that new vibration raise your current vibration even higher, wider, brighter.

- Allow this new higher vibration to change the older heavier, denser patterns/vibrations of your *bodymindspirit*.

- Manifest the *new you* into the world.

As with everything else in this book, you can revisit different exercises. You can also do a ceremony whenever you want to mark a moment of transformation and initiation.

As Marianne Williamson wrote, "Be the change you want the world to be."

Honoring you!

Change can be invigorating, empowering, disorienting, confusing, delightful, and scary as hell.

Now that you are truly different, you might find it difficult to respond differently to situations while your loved ones retain old expectations of you. They only know the old you and your old reactions. Even when our loved ones root for us to change, the actual reality of our change can challenge them. Change is difficult for everyone. We are creatures of habit and sometimes have a hard time accepting change even if it's for the better.

Be gentle with yourself. Remember all your gifts, and honor all of who you are — not the old story people believe about you.

CREATE

MAGNIFICENT YOU

Set up your painting space. Create your sacred space. Ground yourself. Ask for a foundation blessing.

- Ask your creative heart for a word, phrase, or a simple image that you can say, visualize, or feel, one that reminds you of the *new you.*

- As you go through each day, focus on that word or image to remind yourself of the new you. Put that word or image everywhere: your car, house, refrigerator, even on your bathroom mirror. You can request that your friends not ask you to explain that word or image. Or you can tell them the words or images are a reminder for you to be true and authentic in your life.

- Just like a journal, you can share your reflections and creations or keep them to yourself. You are in control of your heart's dreams, desires, and personal secrets. Honor yourself by sharing only what you want to share.

Creative Spiritual Practice

Moment to moment, being present with what's in front of you, accepting all the wild and woolly parts of yourself is a *spiritual practice*. The act of being creative allows you to accept all parts of who you are. Every day, every moment, every breath, you are magnificent, as you effortlessly shine like the stars above you. Regardless of how you feel at any given moment—you are *shining*—because you are spirit in a body enjoying a physical life. You are filled with love from the Universe, the Creator, the Divine.

Your dreams matter. What you daydream about can become reality. Believe in your dreams, not the dreams that society creates for you.

Invite yourself to live fully and presently in *your truth*.

This creative process takes you on a journey back to your magnificent being. You have unraveled and examined all the stories that have limited you. You have remembered your relationship with the energy around you. Filled up with your power, you have moved all that knowledge through your senses to balance your *bodymindspirit* muscle memory to hold your magnificence.

You will change the world by being fully yourself.

Your loving creation

The great LOVE from the Divine, Source, Creator, God/dess that brought you into this world in this body was present before your birth parents conceived you.

Some cultures believe you're a part of the Creator in body, some believe you come into this body only once, others believe that you keep coming back into this body gathering experiences. Whatever you believe, right now you are in a body having this extraordinary human experience.

CREATE

THE LOVE THAT MADE YOU

Take your time and set up your space.

Create a creative womb that will hold you and all the love that is in and around you.

Ground yourself.

When you are ready, put on some ambient music. Robert Rand's "Wavepool" is my favorite.

In this journey—visualize, open up all your senses, see the love, *feel* the love, *hear* the love, allow that love to permeate every cell of your body, to fill your energy fields with love.

- Go to your healing spirits and your guardian energy. Ask for a foundation blessing, then ask them to show you all the love that went into your creation.

- Take all the time you need to experience the love that *sparked* your creation that is *still* present inside you.

- When you are vibrating with this love, ask your creative spirit to bring that energy, that love, into the world with paint on paper (sound or dance).

To experience this love transforms all the gifts you have received during this process and brings you back *full circle.* Back to the truth of you. The magnificence of you. The heart of you.

Know your heart.

Love your life!

Your sacred creation

Your painting is a representation of Love: Love from the pregnant void that brought you into the world, the love of your helping spirits, the Elements, and the Web of Life. This sacred creation is a representation of *You*: your truth, the beautiful parts of you, and the many energetic layers of you.

It is *YOU*: your vibration, your dreams, vision, purpose, and light.

Shamanic art is not a representation of healing; it **is** powerful and profound healing power.

CREATE

MAKE IT SACRED

Set up your painting space. Create your sacred space.
Ground yourself. Ask for a foundation blessing.

• Feel all that love-light vibration shimmering, buzzing,
  singing inside you and around you.

• See, hear, feel your love-vibration expanding outward.

• Experience that vibration more and more fully as you
  expand outward, meeting other love-lights.

• Notice your vibration getting bigger until it becomes
  one with the love-light vibration of the Spirit That Lives
  In All Things.

• Breath that oneness in. Know that you are that
  Oneness.

• Now, let all those sensations, that love-light vibration,
  move from your heart onto paper with paint.

• Paint your love-light vibration. See the shimmer as you
  paint.

• Feel that vibration transcending paint and paper.

• Let it be the powerful and profound healing power that
  it is.

• Let this painting be the synthesis of all the love, the
  healing, the discoveries that reclaiming your creative
  soul has brought forth to empower you to be the gift
  that you are.

• Let this painting BE *love-light vibration.*

Here are a few ways to work with your sacred creation:

- Hang it in a place of honor, place it on your altar.

- Take a photograph of it and make small prints of it.

- Make it your screen saver.

- Place tiny prints of your creation all over your house.

So every time you see your *love-light vibration* you will resonate, shimmer, and shine, echoing out into the world, sharing your love-light with the world.

Be Shiny ... Glow

What is the light that is inside you and all around you?

The transformative alchemical gift of *Painting the Landscape of Your Soul* is to lighten up and essentially transmute the dense patterns of who you were *into* the light, bright, golden energy that you *are*, aka your **glow**.

CREATE

GLOWING YOU

Set up your creative space with the intention of fully experiencing your transformational self, your **glow**.

Ground yourself. Ask for a foundation blessing.

- As always, don't guide it or direct it, let your glow fill you fully.

- Let that glowing you fill the space all around you.

- Notice how you feel when you are glowing from the inside out.

- Let that light-filled vibration move your body, hands, and brush.

- Paint the new glowing you.

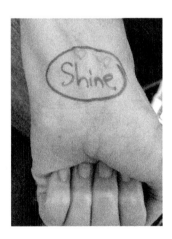

Spreading the Joy

You must enshrine in your hearts
the spiritual urge towards light and love,
Wisdom and Bliss!

— Sri Sathya Sai Baba (Indian guru)

Continuing Explorations to Keep You Shining On

You can go through the exercises in this book over and over again. Or you can choose the ones that call you at a particular moment. Each time you do an exercise you will get new information that takes you deeper into knowing your true, amazing, glowing self. Here are a few explorations for special occasions.

Honoring the turn of the wheel

The turning of the seasons is often likened to the turning of a wheel. It is important to be mindful of the shifting seasons around you and how those shifts are reflected in your being. (As above, so below; As within, so without)

In the beginning, there was nothing. God said, "Let there be light!" And there was light. There was still nothing, but you could see it a whole lot better.

—Ellen DeGeneres (contemporary American comedian)

Winter and summer solstice: We began as agricultural people who followed the seasons for planting, harvesting our food and tending to our herds. Our roots come from the rhythms of the earth. Whether we are aware of it or not, we still follow the rhythms of the earth, the turning of the wheel, the turning of the seasons.

A great way to reconnect with the change of the season is to invite your creative muse to teach you about that season using color, shape, and form.

As the year progresses, as the wheel turns, two solstices — winter and summer — mark the longest night and longest day. In all cultures, celebrations mark this turning of the year. In the northern hemisphere, the winter solstice is on December 21. It's the shortest day and the longest night. The time moving toward winter solstice is a time for deep introspection. The summer solstice is on June 20, the shortest night, the longest day, and it's a good time for being in community.* These are generalized statements; I do know some folks whose

*If you are in the southern hemisphere, winter solstice is in June and summer solstice is in December.

seasonal reactions are the opposite of the norm. Respect the rhythm that feels right for you.

Fall and spring equinoxes are the midway points between the solstices, and they mark when day and night are equal. Staying in rhythm with the seasons will create less stress on your *bodymindspirit* thoughout the year.

Another way to think of day/night and the various levels of light is to think about the yinyang symbol. The yinyang symbol, from Taoist philosophy, is a visual representation of the turning of the wheel, around us and inside us. It represents two distinctly different polar energies that cannot exist without each other. The end of the tail in both the black and white areas shows us the pivotal points of fullness (solstices) and impending shifts of light. For instance, if you want to explore your inward/yin/nighttime/winter energy, you can go to the winter solstice energy. The same is true for the outward/yang/day/summer energy.

Yet mystery and imagination arise from the same source. This source is called darkness. Darkness within darkness, the gateway to all understanding.

—Lao Tzu (philosopher of ancient China)

Solstice celebration with paint on paper: The best time to explore the energy of solstice is to paint just before or actually on the solstice itself. Creating and ceremoniously marking these powerful times can be filled with extraordinary learnings: how you ebb and flow, how you move from light to dark to light. Bring your full intention, dreams, and questions to your solstice inquiry. It can be life changing.

Painting during a powerful earth energy shift can align your energy in a way that can only happen twice a year (once for summer, once for winter). Many cultures have celebrations on the solstices. Celebrate in your own unique way. Invite some friends.

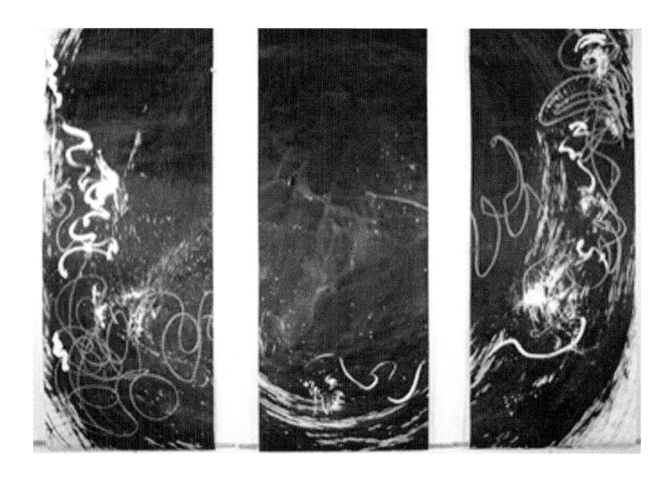

CREATE

PIVOTS OF LIGHT

Set up your painting space. Create your sacred space. Ground yourself. Ask for a foundation blessing.

- Welcome in the Spirits of the Land you are on.

- Welcome the Elements and the directions.

- Make a centerpiece, an altar, and add offerings, flowers, pictures, stones, or anything that will add to your solstice celebration.

- Bring your prayers and your dreams for the next turn of the year—write them down, draw them out, sing them.

- Close your eyes, and in your heart feel your intention to merge with the energy of solstice (winter or summer).

- Let the energy of solstice move you with paint to paper and discover the gifts of solstice energy that are in *you*.

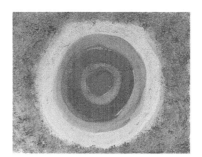

Four Seasons: We have explored the Elements, the moon, the dance of day and night; now lets look at what each season offers you.

The four seasons are summer, fall, winter, and spring. Knowing how you shift from one season to another is paramount to your health. In fact, special seasonal treatments in Asian medicine are done once each season to keep you healthy and aligned. These treatments bring you back into relationship and alignment with that season, reminding your being about the movement and the quality of each season — inside and outside of you. They reconnect you with the rhythm of life, again and again, year after year.

The best times to connect with seasonal energy are at the very beginning of each season (to prepare) or at the height of the season (to experience fullness). The solstices and equinoxes mark the beginning of the seasons in the Western calendar and are considered the peak of the season in the Asian calendar.

In the Northern Hemisphere:

(Solstice)	December 21 / Winter	June 21 / Summer
(Equinox)	October 21 / Fall	March 21 / Spring

In the Southern Hemisphere:

(Solstice)	December 21 / Summer	June 21 / Winter
(Equinox)	October 21 / Spring	March 21 Fall

CREATE
SEASONAL HONORING

Set up your creative space with the intention to explore the season.

Create your sacred space. Ground yourself.
Ask for a foundation blessing.

- Let the creative process *prepare* you for the upcoming season. Or paint at the height of that season, to know how that season's fullness resonates with you — the pop of spring, the fullness of summer, the brightness of autumn, and the darkness of winter.

- Let your intuitive creative self dialogue with that season's energy, and let it teach you with color, shape, form, and vibration. Be open to anything that shows up. Your wise creative self may not speak to you in ways you expect from that season.

When you engage with the Elements, heavenly bodies, and your helping spirits, the possibilities for inner learning are endless.

We're blessed to have ways to create a deeper connection with The Web of Life and Spirit That Lives In All Things!

Five movements of life: the five elements

Asian societies follow the turning of the wheel with five seasons represented by the five elements, the five movements of life. Unlike the Western calendar that has the start dates of each season marked, the Asian five seasons start when nature around you shifts, so the dates are not always the same.

Wood/Spring: Growth, Vision, Creativity, Distinctions

Starting around Chinese new year, in February, bird's songs change, small bugs come out, sap starts to rise, and foliage greens slightly.

Fire/Summer: Warmth, Compassion, Partnership

This season starts when it warms and flowers go from bud to bloom, about early May.

Earth/Late Summer: Thoughtfulness, Nourishment, Understanding

Days feel endless, timeless, slower, and it seems the fruit has all the time in the world to ripen.

To paint is to experience. To experience is to know.

Knowing brings energy into your **bodymindspirit** and subtle body energies into **balance**.

Metal/Autumn: Inspiration, Acknowledgment, Respect, Righteousness

The light changes, the air becomes crisper, and the leaves start to change. It's time for the final harvest.

Water/Winter: Wisdom, Potency, Listening

It's dark and still. It is colder, and there are no leaves on the trees.

In numerology *five* represents the movement of life versus *four* that represents the stability of life, the four elements. These five elements teach you about the five stages of life and how you flow with each one.

Experience each of these five elements — Water, Wood, Fire, Earth, and Metal in yourself. Explore one at a time. Because this is about a movement of life, start with water and move around the cycle, to learn about that flow in you. As you meet each elemental energy, allow each one to teach you about its energy *in you*, and then begin to balance each one within you, to experience health and well-being year round.

CREATE

THE FIVE MOVEMENTS OF LIFE

There are two ways to learn about the five elements in you.

1. You can paint in any season to learn about and discover that elemental energy inside yourself. For example, you can start today with inquiring into your Water energy — via color, shape, and form. Then next week, explore Wood. The following week Fire, and so on.

2. You can paint *in* any of the five elemental seasons to find a place of balance in you with that element. For example, your can paint in spring, with the intention to explore and balance your Wood energy. There is a similar acupuncture treatment that is done at the beginning of each season to balance that seasonal element in you. For example, when you see the leaves start to change you can paint the element Metal — to explore and balance Metal inside you.

Create your sacred space. Welcome the spirits of the Land you are on. Welcome the Elements and the directions. Ground yourself. Ask for a foundation blessing.

• Make a centerpiece, an altar and add any offerings, flowers, pictures, stones, or anything that will represent your elemental exploration.

• Close your eyes, and in your heart feel your intention to merge with the energy of one of the five elements.

• Then let the energy of Wood, Fire, Earth, Metal, or Water fill you, move you — via color, shape, and form to reconnect with your elemental energy.

La bella luna

How do you feel when you see the moon? Do you feel indifferent? Excited? Mysterious?

The moon is a heavenly body, that is alive and has spirit, just like the sun that influences our unconscious movement through life. The moon regulates the water tides and the tides of our unconscious, emotional lives.

Does your body know when the moon is full? Does the new moon speak to you in dreams? Do you feel the moon around when the sun is out?

CREATE

A LUNAR MEETING

Notice how your creativity changes with a full moon, a new moon, a waning moon, a waxing moon. Take some time to connect with the energy of the moon. You can do short creations nightly for the entire moon cycle. Perhaps, even create in moonlight.

Open your heart and hear what the moon has to say to your creative soul. Let the moon energy share the deep mystery of who you are with color, shape, and form.

Set up your space so that you are ready to create when the moon's tides call.

Create your sacred space. Ground yourself.
Ask for a foundation blessing.

- Let the moon guide your heart.

- Let it guide your intuitive self.

- Let the moon share its energy, its vibration with you. Ask the moon to teach you about yourself.

- Follow the tides, the ebb and flow. Go with the motion.

- Learn about the lunar part of yourself.

Paint your New Year's vision

Culturally, there is a big emphasis on the turning of the calendar year. Perhaps you have even made a New Year's resolution or two.

This New Year, invite your creative soul and the Elements to share with you the gift that you are to bring forth. Let this creative act bring aliveness, excitement, and vision to your *new* year.

Ask the Sacred to bring forth a clear New Year's intention, a vision that you will manifest in the *new year*. Bring your dreams out into the open. Let your dreams be fed by the Elements — Fire, Water, Earth, Air, and *love*.

Let this vibration merge with your desire, your intention and let it come forth with color, shape, form, sound, and movement. Combined, they will add a dynamic spark to your New Year's resolution.

CREATE

NEW YEAR... NEW DREAMS: CREATE

Set up your painting space. Create your sacred space. Ground yourself. Ask for a foundation blessing.

- Settle yourself comfortably.

- Feel where your body meets the *earth*.

- Feel the top of your head meeting the sky.

- Feel the *air* moving around and inside you as you breathe deeply.

- Feel the blood, *water*, moving inside you: feel your muscles, *earth*, shifting; feel the beat of your heart and passion, *fire*.

- As you acknowledge the elements in you and around you, invite them to communicate with your intuitive creative soul.

- Hold your intention for the new year in your heart. Know that the energy, resonance, and vibration of your intention will be expressed in your own unique creative way.

- Be open to what appears.

You are not alone, let your muse, your helping spirits, the Elements help you evoke the exact vibration to inspirit the new year.

Paint your birthday blessing!

When you were born, you brought your unique light to this world, and started your Earth walk. Thank you! Your day of birth should not pass without a celebration.

Invite your creative muse to share with you, your gifts and blessings for the following year. Let the knowing unfold, don't hold back.

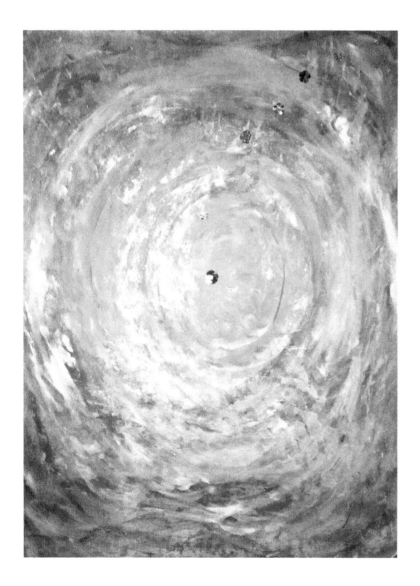

CREATE

BIRTHDAY BLESSINGS ... A GIFT FROM THE ELEMENTS

There is a birthday blessing for you from your wise inner self. Paint it. In this exploration you can ask the Elements to share your birthday blessing, from an elemental vibration perspective.

Set up your painting space. Create your sacred space. Ground yourself. Ask for a foundation blessing.

- Settle yourself in comfortably.

- Feel where your body meets the *Earth*. Feel the top of your head meeting the sky. Feel the *Air* moving around and inside you as you breathe deeply. Feel the blood, *Water* moving inside you; feel your muscles, *Earth*, shifting; feel the beat of your heart and passion, *Fire*.

- Connect with your heart and ask the spirit of Fire to share the vibration of your birthday blessing — via color, shape, and form. Do the same with Water, Air, Earth, Above and Below.

- Let that birthday blessing vibration fill you up. Let the paint flow, brush to paper, leave the story aside — your judgements aside, and let the blessings flow.

You don't have to know what it all means; the Elements will *transmit* your blessing via your inner self, reflect back to your sacred anatomy, and raise your vibration so you can *BE that Blessing.*

Shine. And happy birthday!

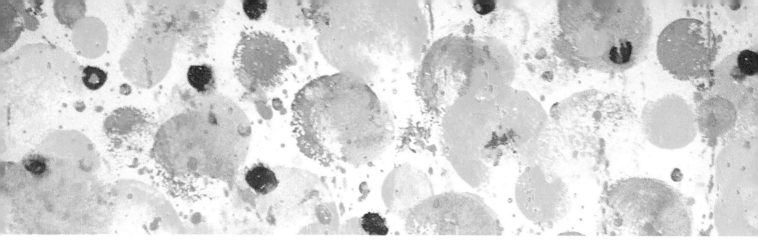

Forty days of being creative

The number *forty* has historical references to it, and although I could not discover where the importance of forty started, it does take a human embryo forty weeks to come to full term. Forty seems to be a transformational passage of time—forty days and forty nights, forty winks, forty days of lent. If you look at fasts, diets, exercise routines, spiritual transformational retreats, forty is the number that shows up over and over again. So it seems fitting that if you invite the creative process into your life for forty days straight, you will change your neural pathways to make a positive change in your life.

Would you like to allow your creative voice to be present in your life every day?

This is the forty-day invitation to expressing your creativity daily. As you know, when you express your creativity, your heart becomes more joyous, smiles arise, and stress disappears. Commit to a creative practice for forty days in a row. Work on one creative piece for the next forty days. Commit to one minute or more a day, which you can do no matter how busy you are. You just need to say *yes*.

One mark, one image, one sound, one word a day will allow you to feel more alive. Invite a friend to join you.

CREATE

FORTY DAYS OF CREATIVE BLISS

Choose the medium, whatever excites you. Remember, this will be for forty days, so you might need to travel with your supplies. For example, paper, a drawing tablet (such as smart phone or tablet), cardboard to collage on, something to knit, needlepoint, spin, or sew. I know I am focusing on the two-dimensional world, so if you are a three-dimensional type, by all means go with what makes you happy.

But here's the thing — you need to add to your one creative piece *daily*, a mark, a word, a stitch, a note. You can layer over your previous days' work, but don't remove anything or cover any of your additions because you don't like them. Let your intuition guide you. Remember to focus on process, not the end result. There is no right or wrong, just forty days that can birth a new creative habit.

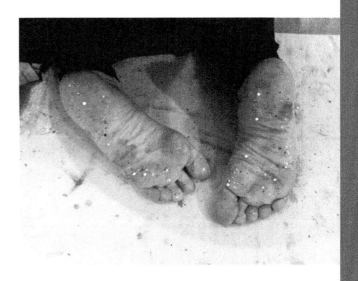

CHAPTER

15

Gather Your Posse

Until now, you have been creating in your private space. Enlisting a creative community can also support your growth, in a powerful and truly healing way. Sure, there is something wonderful and centering about painting alone. Creating alone is a great opportunity to listen deeply and contemplate what shows up. Yet sometimes when you're alone, if the saboteur shows up, you may decide you are done for the day, get a cup of tea, or find a thousand other distractions to call it quits. Yet the saboteur is patient, will wait until you return, and will show up again when you resume your work.

Creating in a group can be a very different experience. Although the group still follows the same guidelines as when you create alone, there's more energy in a group. Each person in the group rides their own wave and rides the wave of the group's collective. Plus, a creative posse won't let you walk away when the saboteur shows up.

I encourage you to find some friends to gather once a week, once a month, or every full/new moon. If coming together in person doesn't work, you can find an online buddy to work with using Internet video. If Wi-Fi is not available, you can have a creative phone call buddy, to meet regularly with or to call when you get stuck.

Creating in community is powerful, but not necessary. However, once you start telling your friends what you are doing, and they see the transformation in you, they will want to join in.

Remember, you can meet anywhere. After all, it is only kids' paints and paper.

Create your posse

Opening the circle is an important step to signal that you have entered into your creative time and left your day-to-day routine and blah-blah-blah-chatty-chatty mind behind you for a few hours. As a group, you can pick a theme to start with — you can revisit any of the exercises in this book or look at the continuing journeys listed on my website for new inspirations.

You can alternate who *leads* the circle, lights the candle or incense, smudges, reads a poem, tells a joke, or otherwise gets the group going by way of the ritual you have chosen.

I suggest that you start each circle by checking in with each other.

What is your greatest aliveness? As the group gathers in circle, before you paint, check in with each other. What is the one thing that is in front of you right now? Is it a dream, something that has been on your mind, or how you are feeling? As a group, listen without any comments, suggestions, or offering ways to fix the situation. Just open your heart and let the person say what is their truth in that moment. Allowing a person to speak without interruption builds trust in the

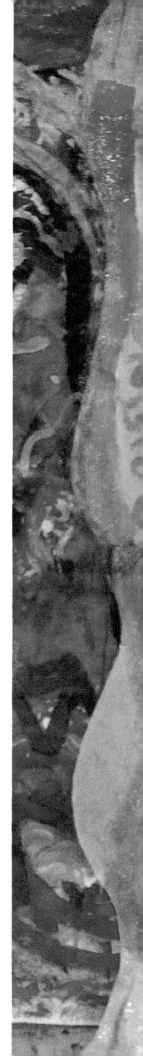

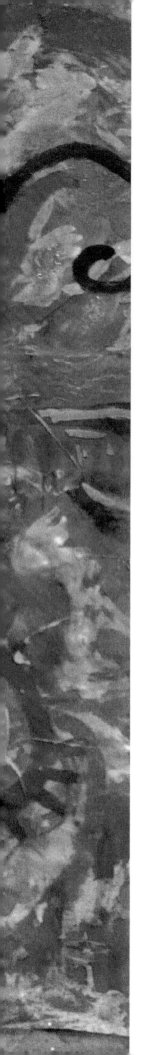

group, which allows you to be freer during your creative time — and most likely, in life, too. Set a limit on the opening, or else you could talk all day. Sessions are best in three-hour blocks:

- Opening and checking-in — Thirty minutes for everyone to check in and share

- Creative time — Two hours

- Closing — Fifteen minutes

- Clean up — Fifteen minutes

As a creative community, support each other as your energy intertwines, ebbs, and flows, tears flow, and anger flares. Stay in your process, and send love to your fellow group members. I recommend that one person be the support person for anyone who needs help. Let one person each painting session hold that role. If all of you feel like you are the support person, no one will fully surrender to their own process.

Procedures for unsticking and questions for the support person to ask:

- *What was the last thing you did before you got stuck?*

- *How did that make you feel?* Be careful not to get caught up in the story. Stay in the present feeling state.

- Ask the painting *what are three more things you can possibly do?* Watch, and listen for the most excitement or the most resistance.

- Focus on the very next mark.

Please remember: Keep the space safe and sacred and don't comment on the paintings. (verbally or nonverbally)

Close the circle before your posse leaves for the day. It's good to close the circle to conclude the gathering. That can be as simple as holding hands, closing your eyes, and speaking one word that is in your heart out loud to the group. Just like your creative process has its own rhythm, so will each group. Open and trust your hearts and let the energy flow.

Radical Rotations

This group exercise radically explores the concepts of process-not-product and nonattachment.

Start by creating your community space as you feel guided. The support person for that session will set a timer for twenty-five minutes. When the timer ends, everyone moves to the painting to their right. If possible, as the support person don't let the group know the plan for the session. No surprise, folks create differently if they know someone will be adding to their painting.

When you move to a new spot, take in the energy of the painting in front of you. Let that energy resonate within you, and first, start responding by using the colors at that station. How does it feel to try on someone else's colors? To work on someone else's painting? If you get the call to use different colors, go ahead, follow your gut. The painting in front of you is no longer the other person's creative process, it's yours. What is important now — is to trust your intuition (your gut, your heart) and respond to what is right in front of you. Add your voice, by way of your mark, on someone else's expression, without

losing yourself. Are you commingling with the energy in front of you? Or are you still doing your own thing on top of someone's painting? Did you go back to your old ways of responding? Or are you letting that painting's energy teach you something new?

Keep alternating to the next painting every ten minutes, until you are back to your original painting. Notice how you feel as you go from one painting to the next. How do you feel mingling with the vibrations of others? Was it harder for you to connect with some and easier with others? Did you hesitate to make a mark on someone else's painting? Were you freer, or more careful?

Once you are back to *your* original spot, how do you feel as you take in the energy of your painting? Continue your conversation with *your* original painting, interact with all those marks, colors, and shapes layered on top of your painting. What does that feel like?

The mixing of and responding to other's energy in your day-to-day life is much like your experience in this "Radical Rotations" exploration. This is what happens when you meet new people, when you teach or speak to a group. Do you hold onto your idea, your vision, or do you integrate with the group? Do you lose yourself? Do you go back to your same old patterns or are you different?

This exercise is a great opportunity to understand how you interact with group energy, how you trust or don't trust your own process, how you trust the group, and how well you know your boundaries. This happens in life all the time; you have your ideas and reactions, then someone waylays or redirects you. Then you come back to yourself, back to your sovereignty.

Quick Reference

Creating your own creative womb

This is your time, your space to drop down, relax, and listen deeply. Set up your sacred space in any way that is meaningful to you. Make a special area to place objects that represent the elements for you: pictures, words, objects that inspire you. Bring in some flowers or greenery. As always, let your intuition be your guide.

Use all your senses to shift a space from day-to-day ordinary to extraordinary. Here are some suggestions:

- Set up your painting space.

- Ground yourself.

- Light a candle (see).

- Smudge the room with white sage, orange spray, or any other scent that would clear the energy of the room (smell).

- Sing a song or ring a bell (hear).

- Place objects on a small table mat to acknowledge the four elements (Water, Fire, Air, Earth) and the four directions (North, South, East, West).

- Welcome your creative self, your muse, your inner four-year-old, and your playful, fearless, curious self.

- Greet your guardian spirits and any other helping energy that you work with.

- Give a great hug of appreciation to yourself for showing up and giving yourself some you time, some precious self-discovery time.

- Ask for a foundation blessing.

- Listen, respond ... listen, respond ... honor all that shows up.

- May your intuitive creative heart lead you to new discoveries of your magnificent self.

Set up an environment for the Divine to whisper the **truth** of who you are and create it forth.

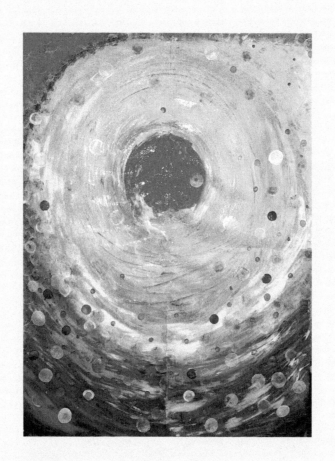

Unsticking

Watch for signs of getting waylaid: Distracted feelings like being bored, hungry, tired, achy; watching the clock, and/or covering previous color, shape, or form because no one is watching (and you don't like it).

"What's next? Now what?" are the first questions to ask your intuitive self when painting. Take the first answer that comes to you. That is the only thing you should respond to at that very moment. Stay in the present. Don't worry if it doesn't make sense or fit into a story. Leave the what ifs or whys for another time.

If you experience body aches or pain in your body, then ask that pain if it has a color, shape, or form. Then ask it where on the painting that mark should go. Sometimes a simple question is all you need to be on your way painting again. Trust that whatever impression shows up it is exactly what you need right now, and keep following the energy.

If you really get stuck and can't seem to get out of your own way, look at your painting with a soft gaze. View it from your feeling place; don't inspect or judge.

- Ask your painting what three, four, or five things can happen.

- Name them or write them down.

- Which one brings a twinkle to your eyes, raises your eyebrows? Which one has the most energy? The most resistance? Surrender to the resistance — that's your next best step.

- Put paint on your pallet and follow the flow of energy.

- Trust the brush. One brushstroke at a time, one breath at a time.

Supply list

I have found that the more expensive supplies are, the less they are used. To use inexpensive supplies gives you the freedom to express, not be limited by frugality, carefulness, cost.

Which paint to use: Use children's liquid tempera paint, sometimes called poster paint. It's nontoxic and water soluble. (Don't buy egg tempera). It's important to have enough paint to really explore color, shape, and form — that's the joy of painting. Buy at least 8 oz. of each color: red, yellow, blue, green, black, and white. There are many places to buy this paint locally or online. You can choose to buy the basic colors and blend them as you paint or purchase a variety of more colors. Six- or twelve-pack basic tempera paint will also do nicely.

Paper: Bristol paper with a vellum finish, sheet size approx. 19" × 24", minimum 80 lb. weight will be just right. It is inexpensive, plus the 80 lb. weight makes it thick and heavy enough to withstand lots of paint. Believe it or not, you can also buy paper from a print shop and it will often be much less expensive than from an art supply store.

Brushes: You can go to your local hardware store and pick up some inexpensive paint brushes, or to your local hobby shop. A brush can be anything that makes a mark or you think would be fun to paint with — sponges, plastic forks, spoons, old makeup brushes. If it calls to you, take it to your studio.

Other things to keep around:

- 1 or 2 plastic containers, like a 32 oz. yogurt container to hold water

- A few plastic takeout containers (top and bottom), an old cookie sheet with sides, plastic tray, or serving platter to use as a painting pallet

- Masking tape to join the paper together (to make bigger and bigger paintings)

- Some old cloth rags (2 or 3)

- Old oversized shirt or apron. (Kid's tempera paint will often wash out of your clothes, but sometimes it can leave light stains.)

- Pushpins or T-pins to hang your paper on the wall while you paint

- Dish soap to clean your brushes and hands

- Optional, but fun to play with, tempera glitter paint/glue, fluorescent tempera paint, oil pastels, colored pencils, and/or glitter

Energy Exercises

Creative Explorations

The essence of all beautiful art, all great art,
is gratitude.

—Friedrich Nietzsche

Grazie Mille

To my mother, Marie, who has always encouraged the creative muse in me, and my father, Bob, who taught me about tenacity. Both of them kept me grounded and more importantly held me with love, no matter where my journey for self discovery led me.

To my Sisters in the Tribe of the Traveling Brush — Corrine, Linda, Kathye, Carolyn, Victoria, and Erica, who love and support me exactly where I am. To Annamarie, Nancy, Mary, and Margaret, whose wise guidance helped me bring my vision into words, not just with paint on paper. To Ann, who heard my call and helped me put this book to words and Barbara who crafted the words into a book. To the Stellarvisions team — designers extraordinaire. To all the amazing people who held the space for me while I talked about birthing this book.

I would like to thank all my teachers. My nonordinary teachers who gifted me with the idea of writing this book. For my teachers in flesh and bone. Sandra Ingerman, for her love and dedication to Shamanism, the planet, and a deep belief that if we change ourselves we can heal Mother Earth. Chris Zydel for her amazing wisdom, vision, and a great sense of humor.

To all the beautiful souls I created with as we inspired each other to follow the truth in our hearts.

To the Web of Life, and my helping spirits who guided me along my way. And to you, the reader, for following your heart, and your desire to be fully alive and create!

Afterword: Advocate for the Soul

I see myself as an advocate for the soul—the soul that wants to vibrate love and joy during its time in this beautiful body on this exquisite planet. It is a blessing to be born into body; to feel all the LOVE that Creator poured into you that sparked your soul into form.

Our senses allow us to experience this world around us on many different levels: Connecting with The Web of Life, connecting to our Helping Spirits, the Elements, and Beings all around us.

Knowing *the truth and divinity of who you are* allows your soul to be expressed freely. Freedom brings joy, love, and happiness into you and then spreads out to the world around you. When you are in your truth, you can be a mirror for others around you who desire the same—to know their truth.

As human beings, we ebb and flow with desires, emotions, and responses. The more you know your truth, the more you realign your subtle energy systems and change your neural pathways to remember the Light Being that you are. You will *inspire* others to shine too.

Yes, we are changing the vibration of the world, one creative act at a time.

Imagination lays the track for the reality train to follow.

—Caroline Cassey

Know Your Heart.
Love Your Life!

www.daminicelebre.com

CPSIA information can be obtained
at www.ICGtesting.com
Printed in the USA
LVOW05s2319190717
541973LV00040B/859/P